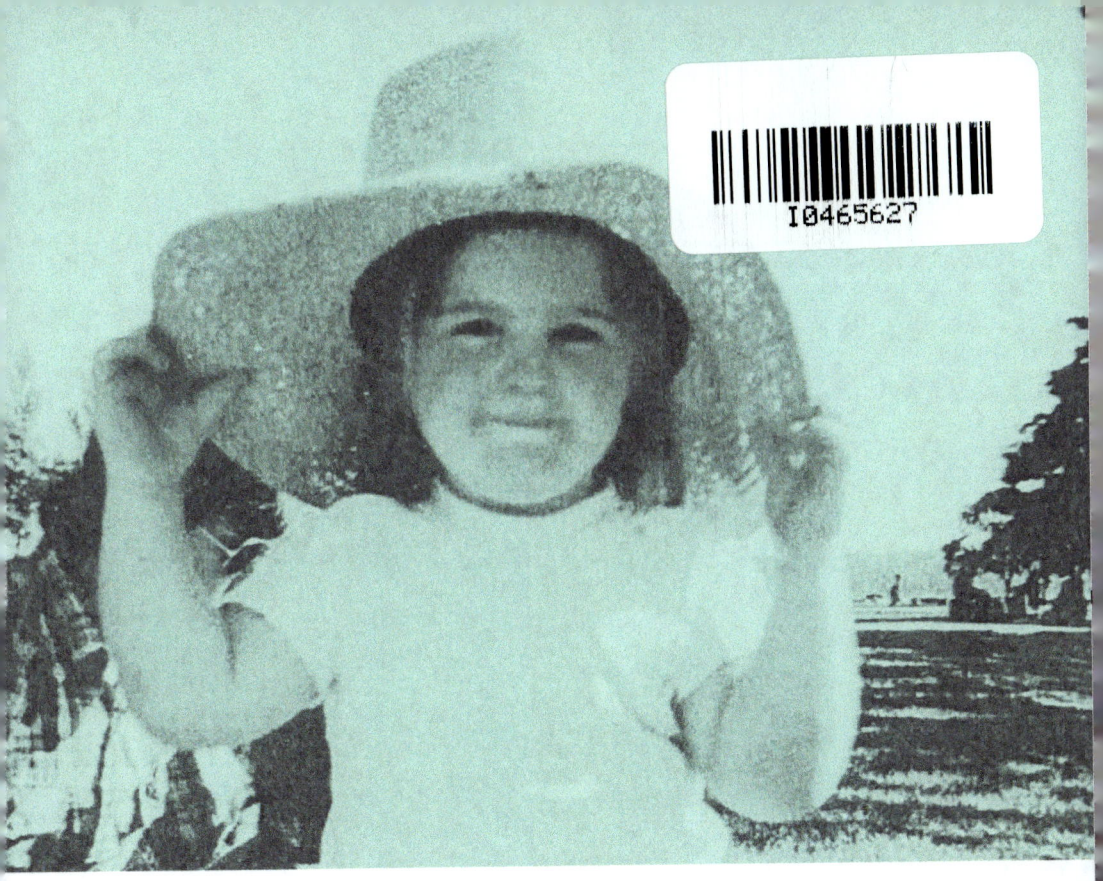

# BE LIKE WATER

## A Visual Memoir

By Juliette Ricci Lagman

Be Like Water / Juliette Ricci Lagman — 1st ed.

979-8-218-48404-0

www.juliettericcilagman.com

lulu.com **lulu**

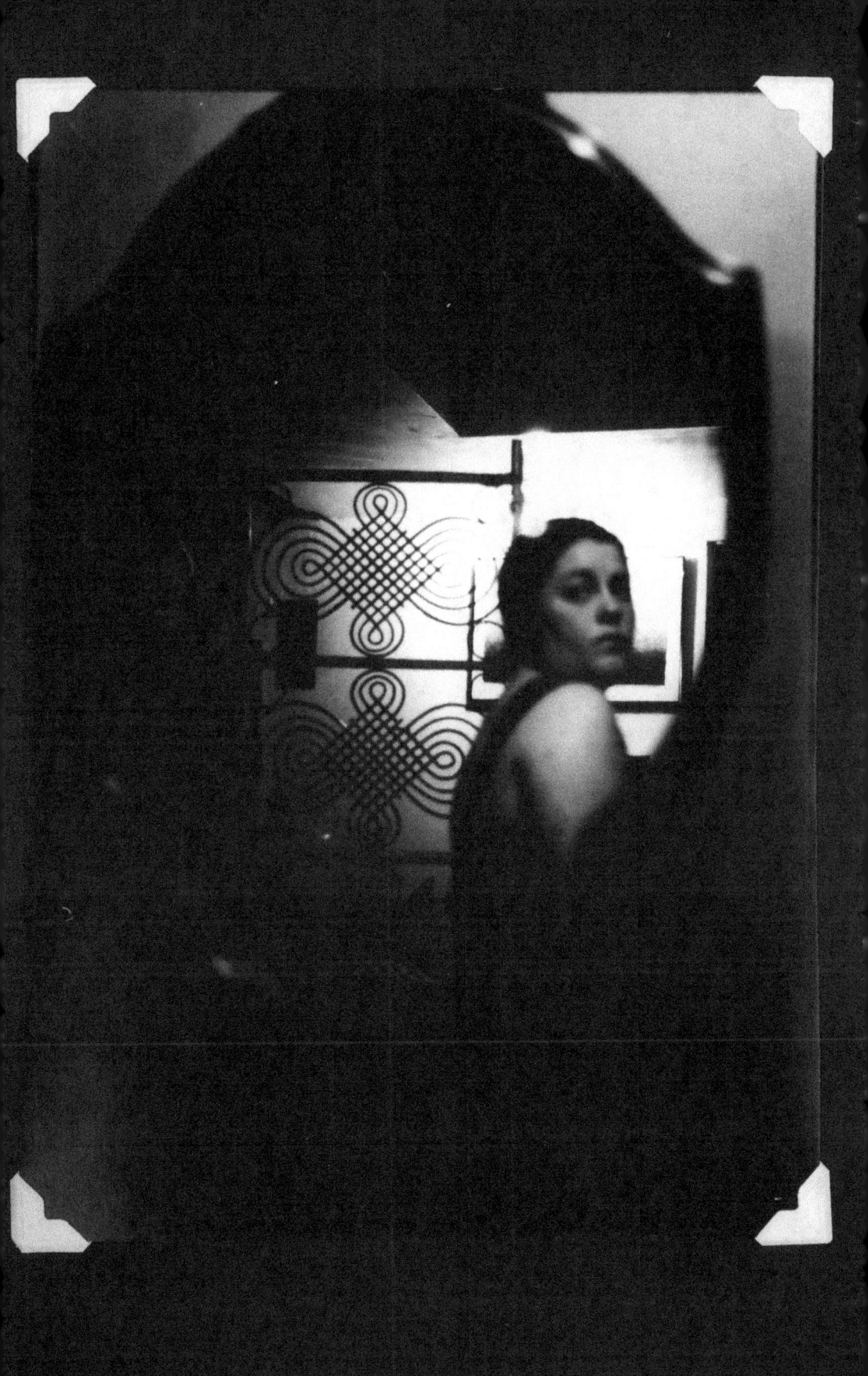

Mom, Croatia 2015

This book is dedicated to every woman
brave enough to write her own story — past,
present, and future.

- Juliette

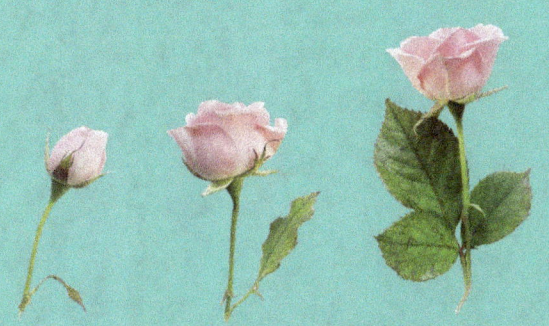

# Part One

*"I'll not abandon myself. Not ever again."*
*- Glennon Doyle*

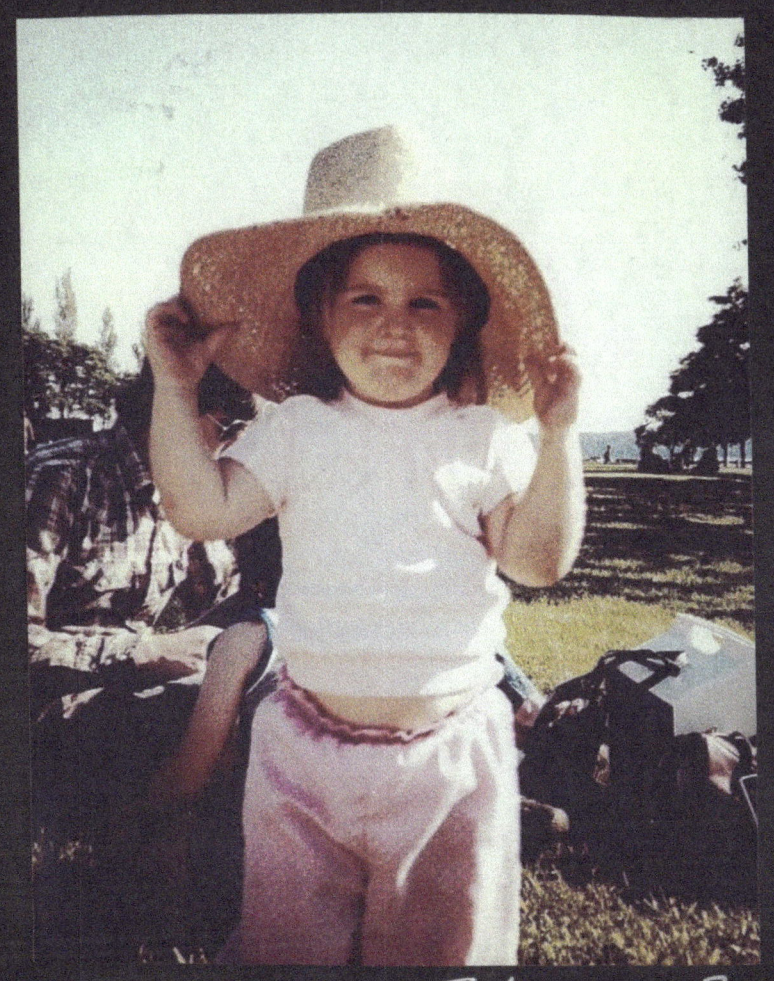

Juliette, age 3

This book is dedicated to every woman brave enough to write her own story – Past, Present, or Future.

*The Letter*

In 1995—

I received a letter from my brother.

He was in college studying music at the time.

The letter was sweet and funny-

in his all caps handwriting.

The most important part of the letter was the
poem he wrote at the end entitled:

"BE LIKE WATER."

I should have framed that letter the first day
I received it.


My brother saw who I truly was -

"Beautiful, Powerful, and Cool."


He saw what I should have seen from the
beginning

but


I was too busy
always protecting myself
trying to survive
to believe
know
and accept the truth
of who I was.


All this time I was learning to swim, but too
afraid to jump in.

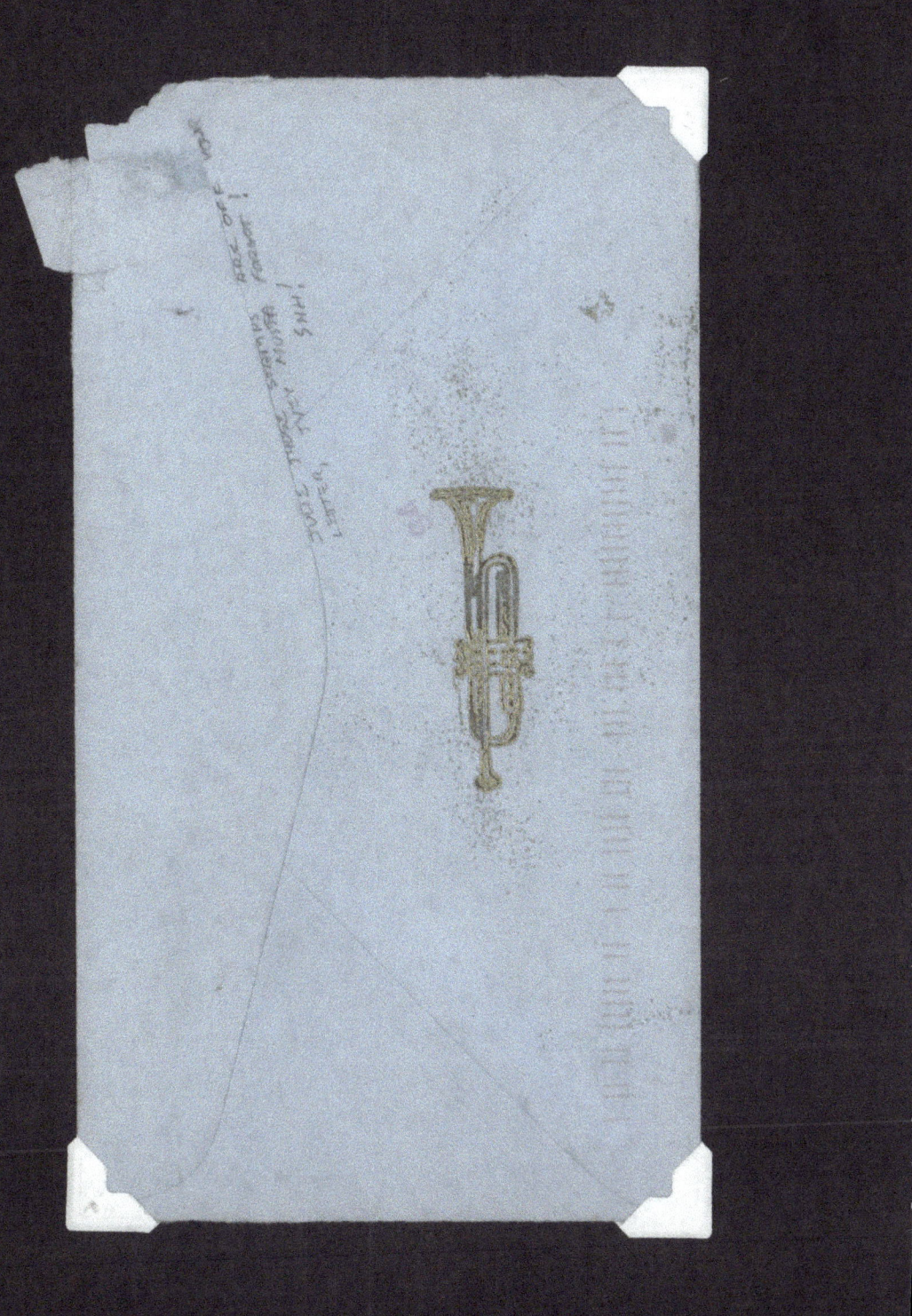

I THINK, OF COURSE THAT EXPRESSIO[N]
SUCH AS JOY AND HARMONY ARE
SPIRITUAL AND THEREFORE REAL. SO
I GET MYSELF A HEAPING BUCKET[FUL]
FULL OF JOY EVERY DAY.
(SOMETIMES I TAKE TWO)
I SEND YOU SOME

WITH NON-DAIRY
WHIPPED TOPPING,

JOEL

P.S. HERE IS A KOAN FOR YOU:
"BEFORE YOUR PARENTS WERE, WHAT I[S]
YOUR ORIGINAL FACE?"

JULIE,
BE LIKE WATER BE LIKE WATER
FLOW TO THE MOST HUMBLE POINT - DOWN.
FLOW OVER UNDER AND AROUND THE
STONES IN YOUR LIFE AND WITHOUT Y[OU]
KNOWING IT, YOUR COOLNESS WILL HAVE
ERODED THE BOULDER TO SAND. IT'S
NOT WORTH TRYING TO MOVE - FOR AS
M.B.E. SAID "IT IS ERROR TO THINK ABOUT
ERROR - OR SOMETHING LIKE THAT. NEVERTHELESS
BE LIKE WATER RECYCLE YOURSELF
FLOW LIKE THE SLICK

"JULIE, BE LIKE WATER BE LIKE WATER FLOW TO THE
MOST HUMBLE POINT - DOWN.

FLOW OVER AND UNDER AND AROUND THE STONES
IN YOUR LIFE AND WITHOUT YOU KNOWING IT YOUR
COOLNESS WILL HAVE ERODED THE BOULDER TO SAND.

IT'S NOT WORTH TRYING TO MOVE - FOR AS M.B.E.
SAID "IT IS ERROR TO THINK ABOUT ERROR" - OR
SOMETHING LIKE THAT.

NEVERTHELESS, BE LIKE WATER, RECYCLE YOURSELF.
FLOW LIKE THE SLICK MASS OF COOL POWER AND
BEAUTY YOU ARE."

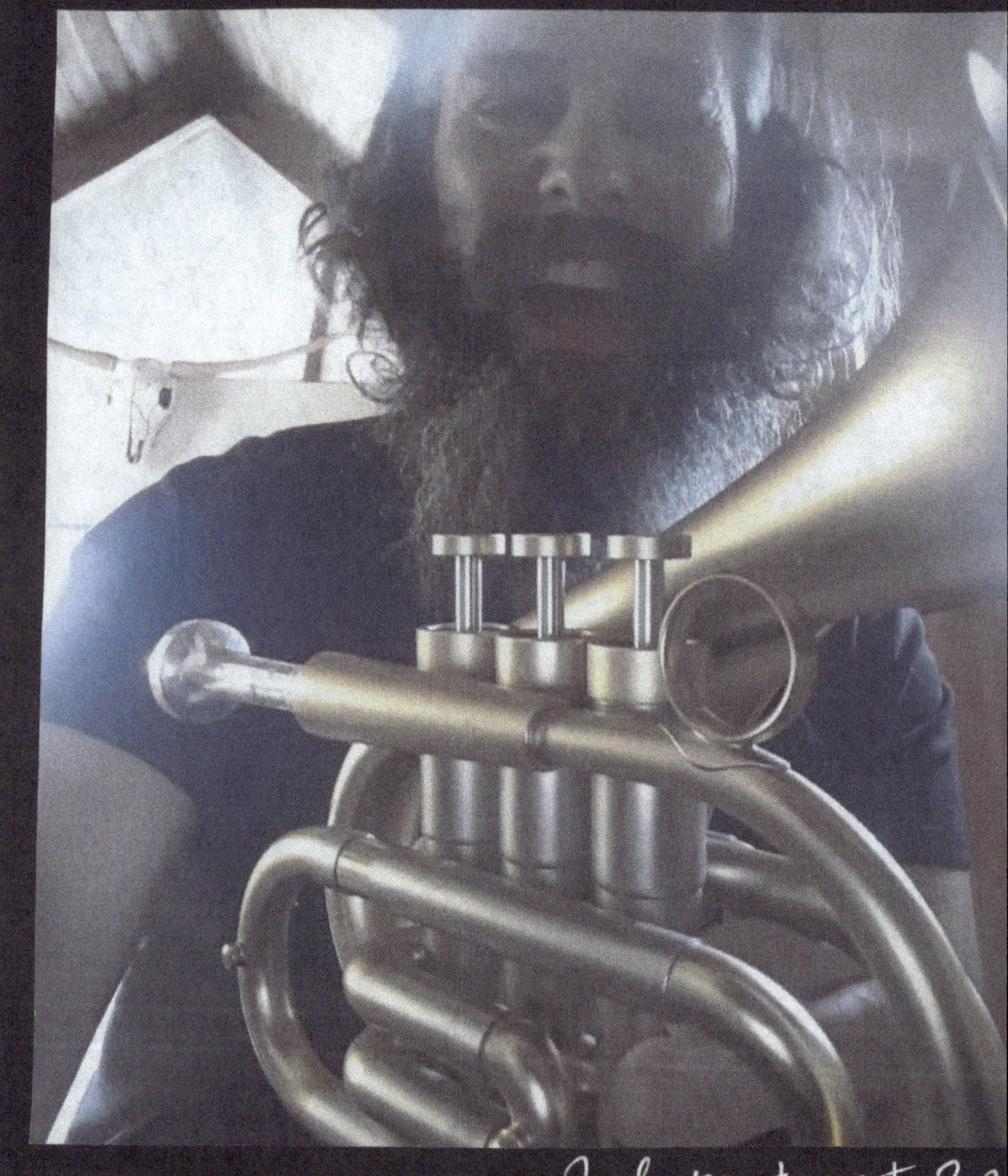

Joel - new trumpet - 202.

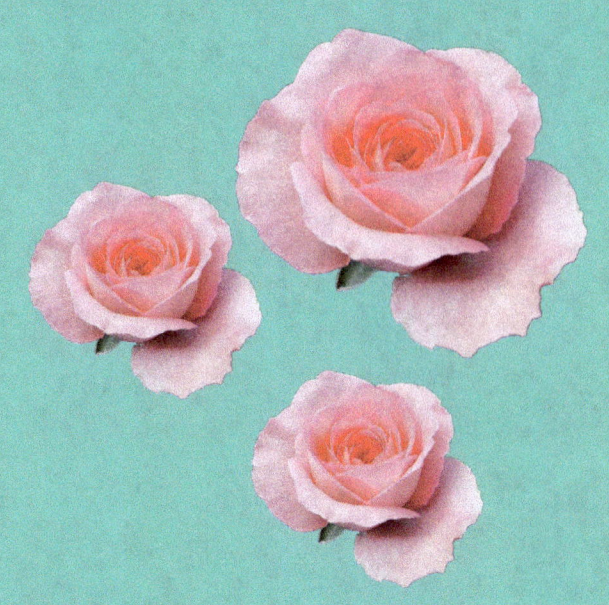

*Dearest Diary,*

I have a round belly.
This round belly has always been.

It carries my
hopes
dreams
fears
and sometimes
**tacos.**

This round belly will always be - I
Love this **belly.**

I Love the girl who walks it around
this Earth
always changing,
but forever the same.

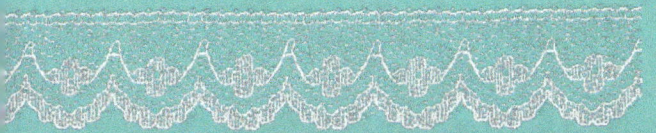

Dear Diary,

I have a round belly. This round belly has always been. It carries my hopes, dreams, fears - and sometimes Tacos. This round belly will always be. I Love this belly. I Love the girl who walks it around this Earth, Always changing but forever the Same.

---

I am at my Stepmoms house for a visit. It's been a little over a year since I've spoken with my mother. I see this photo of myself on the wall amongst the collage of photos of my brother and myself. In this photo - I am three, with sunbleached, frazzled hair - wearing pink with a Huge smile on my face. This is the first time in my life I have Ever looked at a photo of myself and felt Love for that girl

That little girl - feeling so much tenderness, Love, compassion, hope for the future. This is the first time I have felt Love for myself. I realize this is the tip of the iceburg - it is not necessarily an all or nothing situation. I have finally learned to love myself.        Looking at all of these photos in the collage I wonder - what was the problem? Why did I feel such a lack of Love - and abundance of self- loathing?  We look happy, healthy - the way kids are supposed to look.   I guess these things can haunt you.    The dark clouds have lifted.

This is my story of how I got there, and this is just the beginning ...

JM

9/29/2022

I am at my Stepmoms house for a visit.

It's been a little over a year since I've spoken with my Mother.

I see these photos of myself on the wall amongst the collage of photos of my brother and myself.

In this photo — I am three years old, with sun-bleached, frazzled hair.

I'm wearing *pink* with a huge
SMILE.

*This is the first time in my life I have ever looked at photos of myself and felt Love for that girl.*

That little girl

feeling so much

tenderness

Love

compassion

hope for the future.

This is the first time I have felt Love for myself.

I realise this is the tip of the iceberg- it is not necessarily an all-or-nothing situation.

I have finally learned to Love myself.

Looking at all of these photos in the collage,

I wonder:

## what was the problem?

Why did I feel such a lack of Love -

and an abundance of self-loathing?


We look happy and healthy -

the way kids are supposed to look.


I guess these things can haunt you.


The dark clouds have l i f t e d.


This is my story of how I got here,
and this is just the **beginning**.

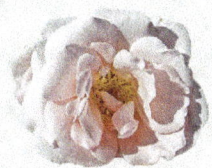 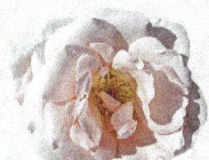 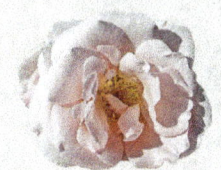

her girl. Don't try to u
because you will lose D
Never undervalue from across the
And never u beauty? who is
you haven't d? I haven't met
she can go. A girl with a
thing.

der cut her wit
ont try to undermine her.
I see you, Seeing my gem.
room. who is that a
that magnificent mine for
k dream is a dangerous

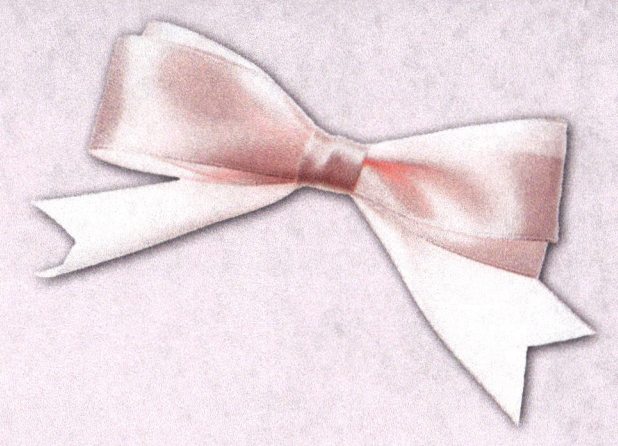

*Trust.*

Trust that what I am telling you is the truth.
I just want to be a free bird -
just like everyone else?
I just want to be *joyful.*
Can you tell me how to do that -
how to be in the moment?
How to be free?
I've been told it's not that hard-
but maybe that was a lie.

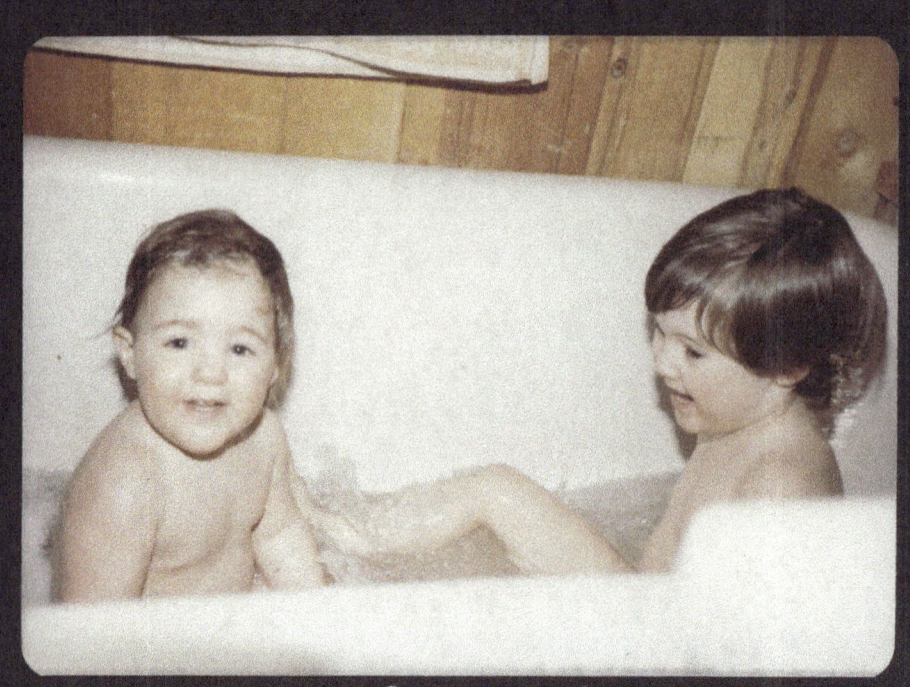

Joel + Julie - Tulalip - WA

Trust. Trust that what I
am telling you is the truth. I
just want to be a free bird —
just like everyone else. I
just want to be happy. Can
you tell me how to do that -
how to be in the moment. How
to be free? I've been told its not
that hard - but maybe that was
a lie.   xo J.

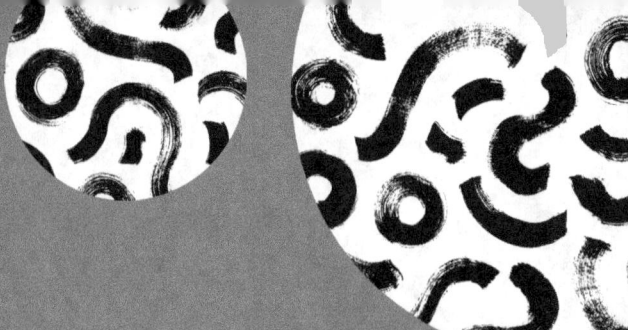

# DEAR DIARY,

I feel like I've been here a thousand times.

Waiting
Waiting
Waiting

Waiting for my life to begin.

## WAITING FOR HER TO LOVE ME

Correction:
Waiting for her to show me and tell me that she loves me.
Waiting to not be an **afterthought.**
Waiting to not be **forgotten.**
Waiting for the day I can be on my own and rely solely on myself.
**Waiting** for the day I can trust myself.

But right now, I'm just waiting for her to pick me up from girl scouts.

Here again, so **embarrassed,** so **abandoned,** so feeling the world shift under my feet every time I think it's ok to stay in one place.

To relax, make a friend, and to let my guard down.

I guess this is why I don't expect much from life.

Dear Diary,

I feel like I've been here a thousand times. Waiting, waiting, waiting. Waiting for my life to begin. Waiting for her to Love me. Correction: to show me and tell me she loves me. Waiting to not be an afterthought. Waiting to not be forgotten. Waiting for the day I can be on my own. Waiting for the day I can trust myself. But right now, I'm just waiting for her to pick me up from Cecil Scout.

Here again, So embarrased, So abandoned - So feeling the world shift under my feet every time I think its ok

a friend and to let my guard
down.

I guess this is why I don't
expect much from life. I don't
ask for much. Life is not reliable.
And as for asking for things, well—
you may as well forget it. I don't
feel I'm worth asking for.

I have come to the source—
to find myself & love myself—To
truly be myself. I have been looking
to fit in and get love every other
way. I have been avoiding doing
the hard things. Do not pass go.
I have tried coming at this—
my mother—every which way, and
nothing has ever evoked that love
and approval.

Now it's time to find it within

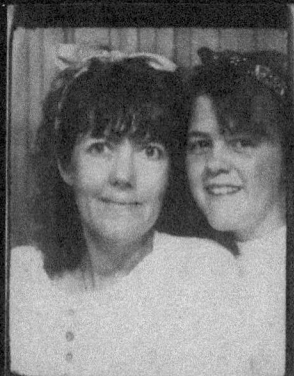

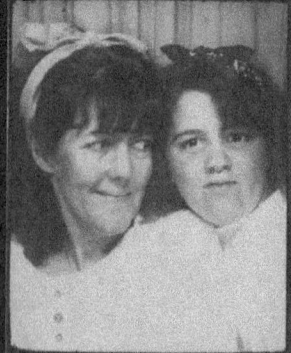

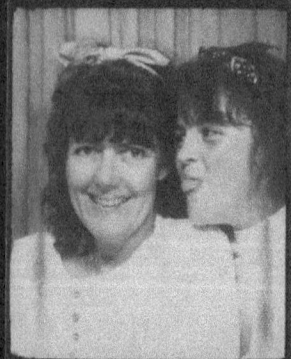

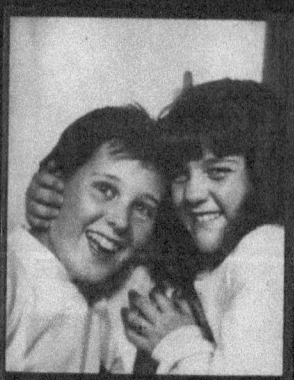

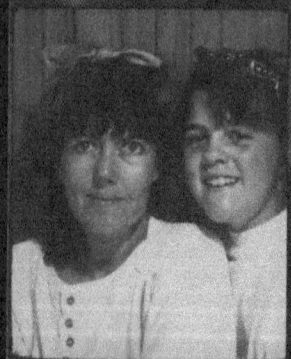

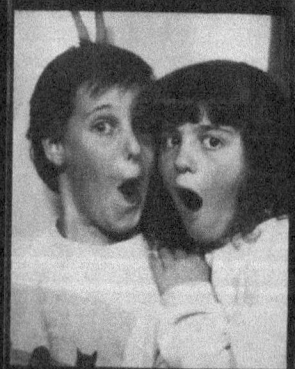

Mom + Julie

Joel + Julie

I don't ask for much.

Life is not reliable.

And as for asking for things, well - you may as
well forget it.


I don't feel I'm worthy of asking for things - I
just end up getting hurt or let down.


I have come to the source- to find myself and
love myself- to truly be myself


I have been looking to fit in and get love every
other way.


I have been avoiding doing the hard work.


Do not pass go.


I have tried coming at this - my Mother - every
which way, and nothing has ever evoked that Love
and approval.


Now it's time to find it within myself - for once
and for all.


xo J

Juliette Ricci
Life Drawing Studios —
Wabash Ave

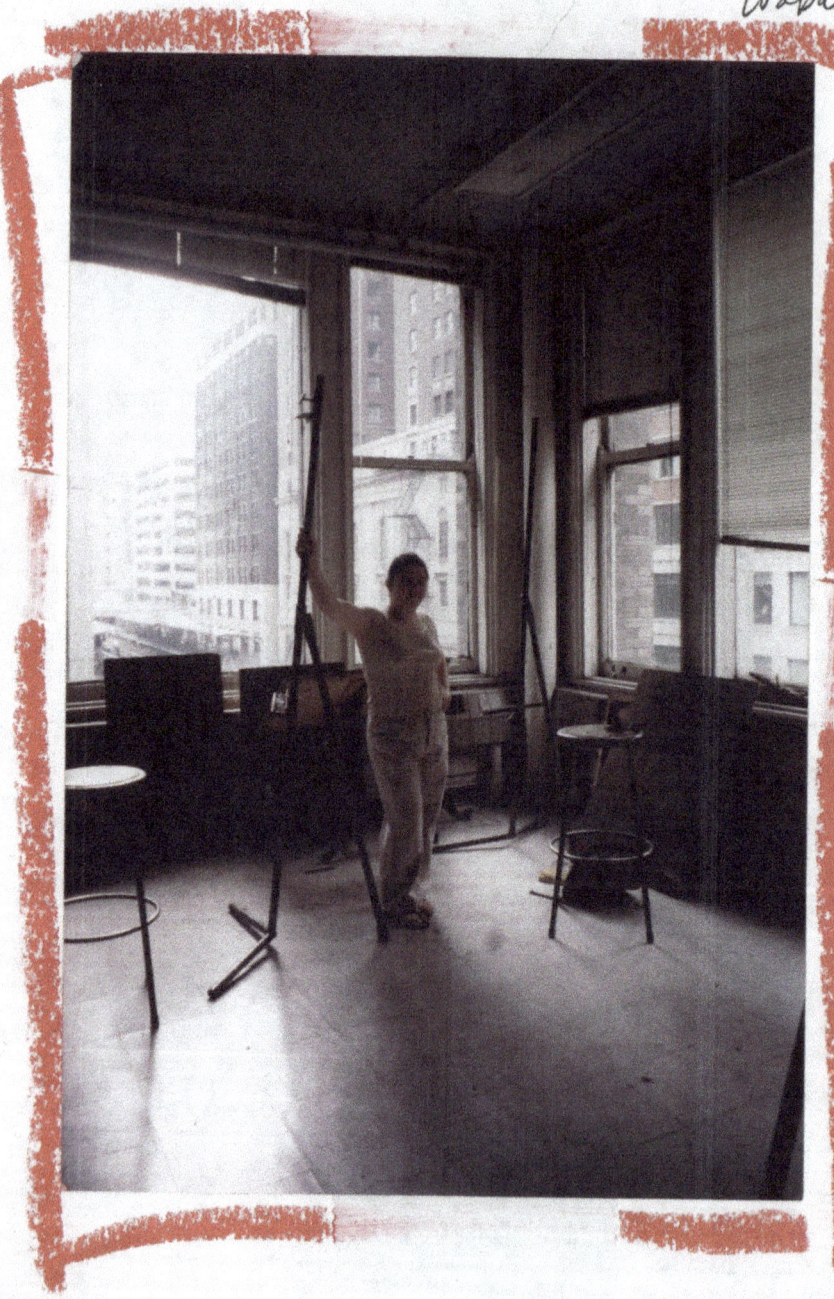

S.A.I.C. ©2000
Chicago, IL

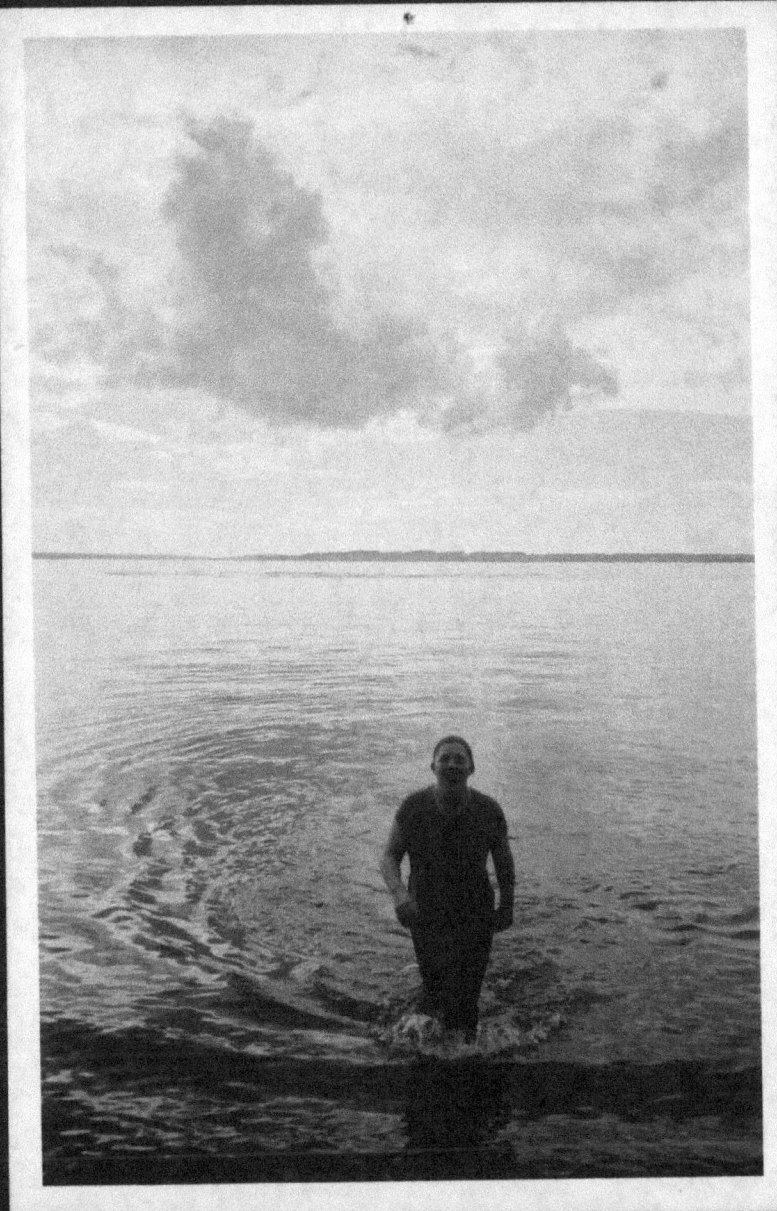

Juliette · carnero island · Photo by RON

All I really want is to set
myself free.
As Liz Gilbert says
        "There is no such thing as
one way liberation."
                xo J.

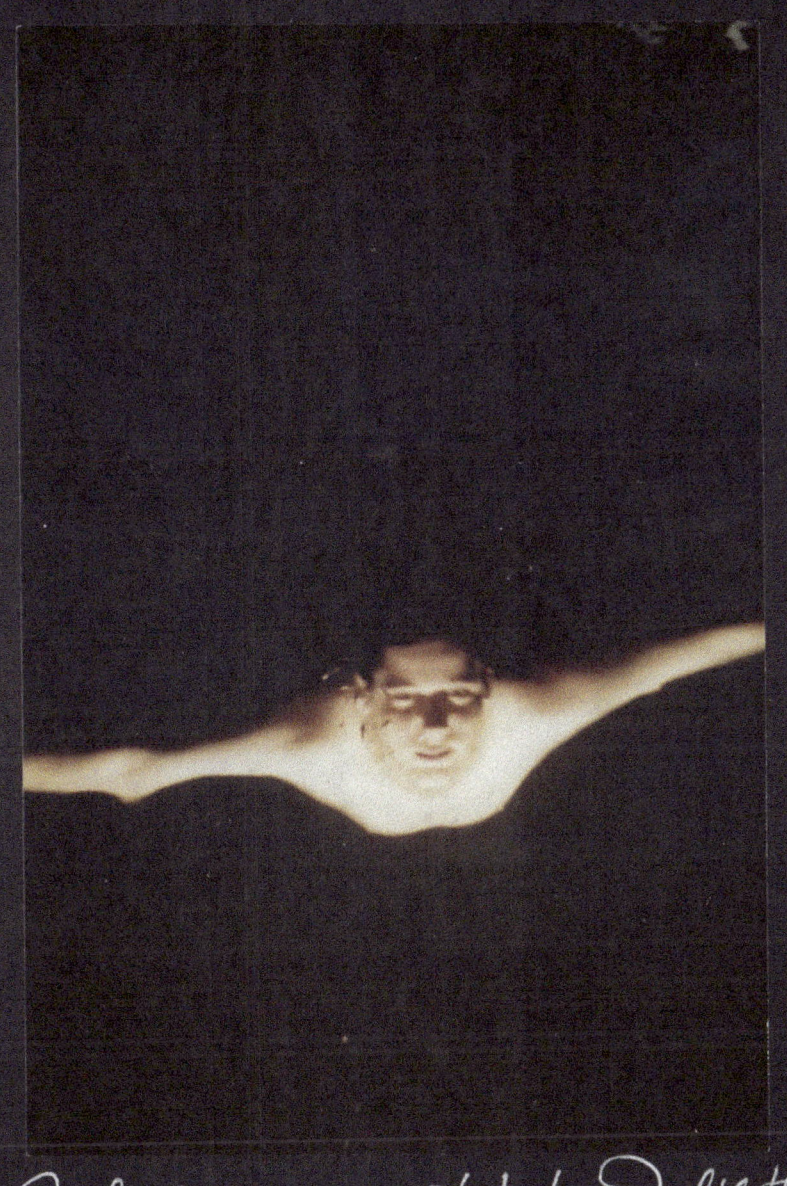

Joel - Swimming - photo by Juliette

Lake Sutherland - April 2023

What would it feel like to be like water - to
flow? To let things roll off your back.  To keep
moving forward, or to rest when you need to?

What would it feel like for no one to question you
- and they just do what you say?

For them to **believe** you, every time you open your
mouth?  That would be nice - not to doubt myself
every time I make a move.

For me - I don't want a life of comfort. I want a
life of *discovery.* I have no problem being scared.
If I am not scared, I'm not trying hard enough.

The other day, I heard an interview with Taylor
Swift. I thought to myself "I wish I had that much
confidence."

It must be nice that her family gave her so much
confidence. Not even support, just **confidence.**

I'm sure she was born with it. But the difference
is that she always had a soft place to land when
coming home from forging her way in the world.

Can I just take a pill, or insert a confidence
battery in me or something?

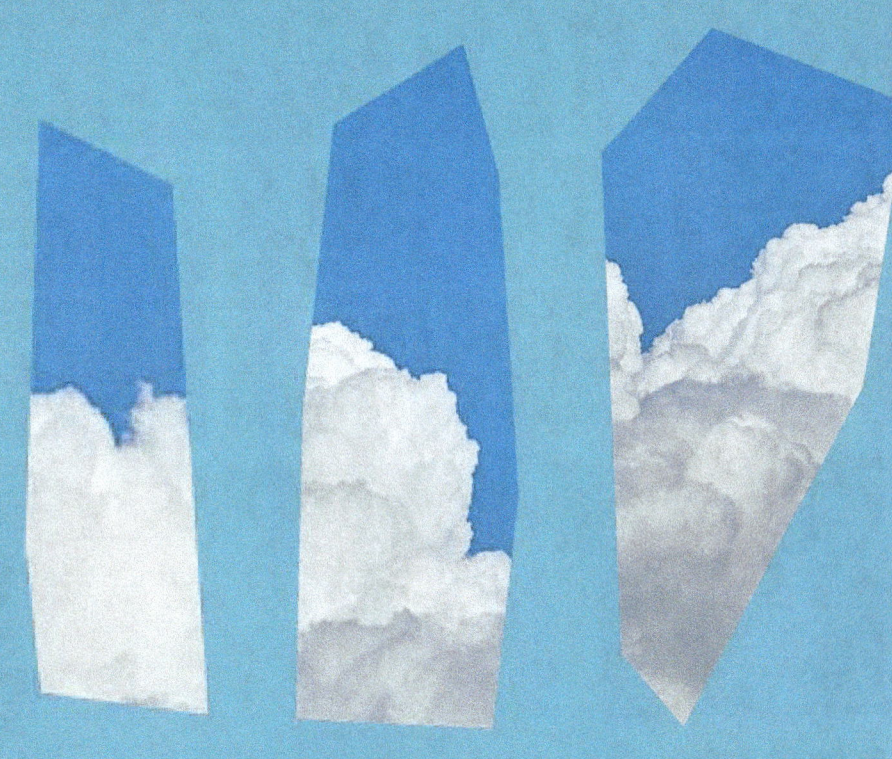

*Dear Dad,*

My middle name is Ricci. If I could take your
name, I would.  If I could have passed on your
name, I would have.

But for now - I will tattoo your name on my skin
- and there it will forever be - as a reminder
that I was loved once.  That I am Loved -
forever from above.

To honour you - the loving one, the flawed
one - the warm one - the one who loved me
unconditionally - with open arms.

Who welcomed me, and asked me how I was - who
taught me the simple pleasures in life.

*Juliette Ricci Lagman 2018*

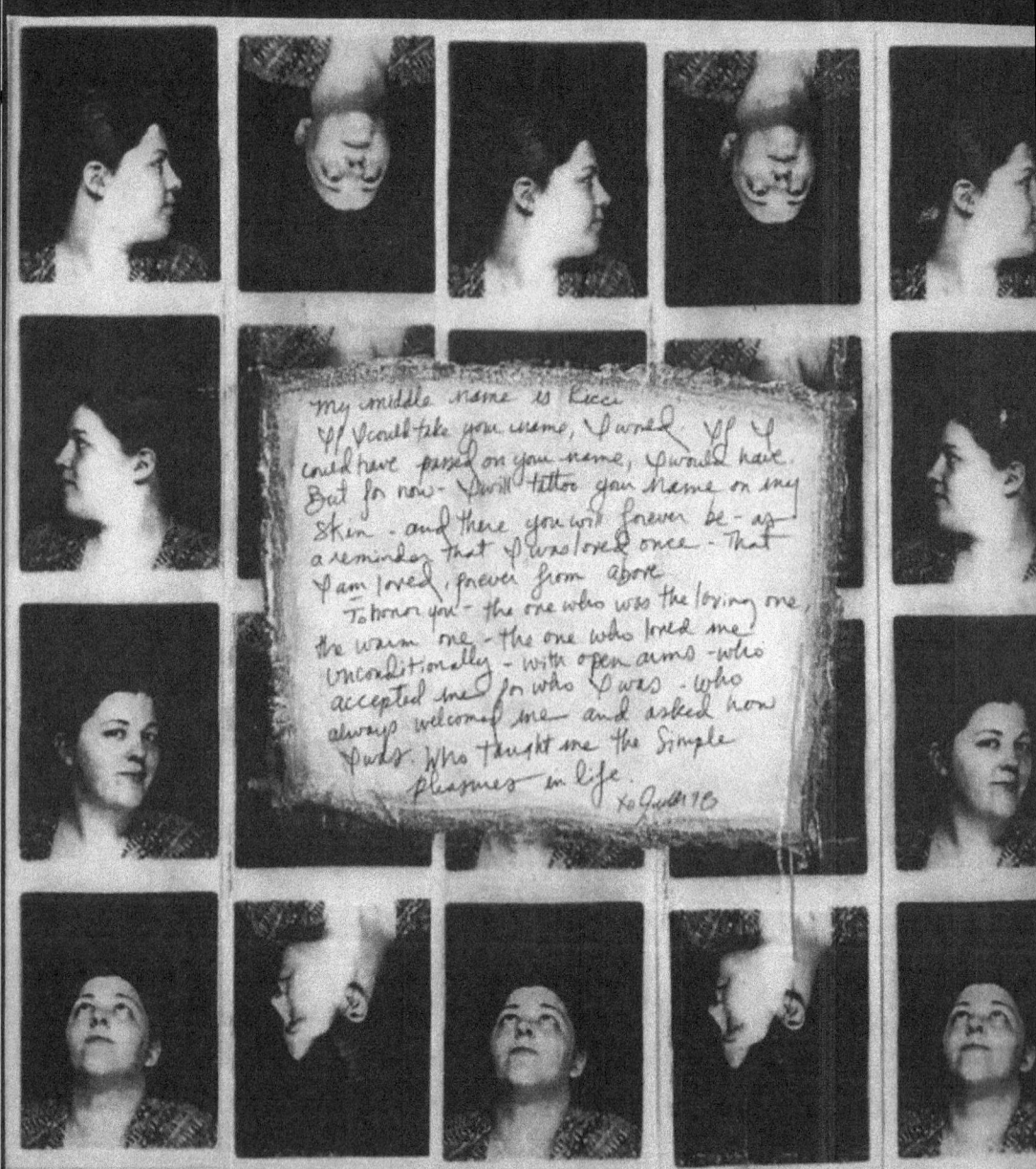

My middle name is Ricci
If I could take your name, I would. If I
could have passed on your name, I would have.
But for now - I will tattoo your name on my
skin - and there you will forever be - as
a reminder that I was loved once - that
I am loved, forever from above.
To honor you - the one who was the loving one,
the warm one - the one who loved me
unconditionally - with open arms - who
accepted me for who I was - who
always welcomed me - and asked how
I was. Who taught me the simple
pleasures in life.
                              xo Jules 98

"My middle name is Ricci" - Juliette Ricci 2

My middle name is Ricci.

If I could take your name, I would. If I could have passed on your name, I would have. But for now - I will tattoo your name on my skin - and here you will forever be - as a reminder that I was loved once - That I am Loved - forever from above. To honor you - the loving one, the warm one - the one who loved me unconditionally - with open arms - who welcomed me and asked me how I was - who taught me the simple pleasures

# DEAR LOVE,

Did I ever tell you about the time my Mom told me I wouldn't be a good mother?

Well, actually

What she said is:

"Your Aunt said you wouldn't be a good Mom."

*Ouch!*

Talk about crushing my heart into a million tiny shattered pieces.

It was my worst fear about myself coming from the one person whose acceptance I *ached* for the most.

I don't know if she said it as a way to motivate me,

I see you, seeing me from across the
room. who is that beauty? who is
that magnificent mind? I haven't met

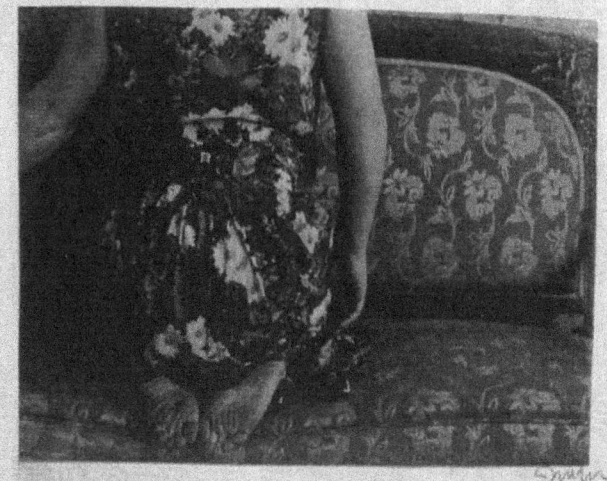

her yet. Don't try to undercut her wit
because you will lose. Don't try to undermine her.
Never undervalue her because she's a precious gem.
And never underestimate her because
  you haven't even begun to see how far
she can go. A girl with a dream is a dangerous
thing.
A girl who believes in herself is even more dangerous

"She Can go" Juliette Ricci 2011

Or why she thought that it would be acceptable to tell me that.
But, she said it after asking me:

**"SO, ARE YOU EVER GOING TO HAVE KIDS?"**

I was 41 at the time.

I was never able to have kids.

Not that we tried hard.

*Dear Love,*

It doesn't matter - all the details of what happened. All I can tell you is that I was born a fragile and very old soul. Possibly neglected and emotionally abused. I was taught to people please from a very young age. Love = survival when you are a child. I broke free when I stopped speaking to my Mother four years ago.

I could tell you story upon story of the times she hurt me - or didn't show up for me. I spent my life searching for her approval and affirmation. Finally I realised I could give those things to myself.

I know as a young woman she loved **art and travel**, she wanted to see everything. She met my father when working for the Forest Service.

It doesn't matter what affliction or afflictions she suffered - all that matters is that I survived and I'm here. And I'm perfect. At least in God's eyes.

win some sort of victory —
Small may it seem.

It's not that I want to 'move on with my life' — I just want to have a good life — that is lived fully — not in fear of everyone + everything. Not a life Shrunk down (lived small) in hopes of merely Surviving. I deserve better than that. My hope in setting an example I can inspire you, dear reader to do the same. If nothing else — enjoy the journey.

'Go confidently in the direction of your Dreams!'

Hi. Eh-hem. Hi There.

If you came here looking for a logical-linear tale from front to back - a tale that makes sense - you came to the wrong place. If you came looking for a magical mystery tour - a mini-roller coaster ride through my brain, heart + guts. You absolutely are in the right place. Line up, get yer tickets ready. You must be this high to go on this ride. You know the saying - 'Sometimes things can only be understood backwards.' Well, here it is - upside down, backwards and from all angles. My true intent with making this book is to heal, and take folks on my healing journey. I don't expect to have all the answers - but I do have a fair amount. My hope + prayer by putting all of these amazing answers in one place is to make things

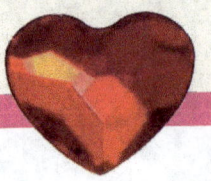

Eh-hem, Hi There.

If you came here looking for a logical, linear tale from front to back - a tale that makes sense then you came to the wrong place. If you came looking for a magical mystery tour, or rather a mini-roller coaster ride through my brain, heart, and guts - well, then you have absolutely come to the right place. Line up, get your tickets ready, you must be **THIS** high to go on this ride. You know the saying "Sometimes things can only be understood backwards."

Well, here it is - upside down, backwards, and from all angles. My true intention with making this book is to heal and share my healing journey. I don't expect to have all the answers, but I do have a fair amount. My hope and prayer by putting all of these amazing answers in one place is to make things a bit clearer, and finally win some sort of victory.

Small may it seem. It's not that I want to move on with my life, I just want to have a good life and some peace. A life that is lived fully, not in fear of everyone and everything. Not a life shrunk down and lived small in hopes of merely surviving.

I deserve better than that. We all do. My hope in setting an example - is to inspire you, dear reader, to do the same. Live life fully, loudly, passionately, and as daring as you can imagine. If nothing else, enjoy the journey.

Touch the Sky . . . Self-portrait . Occ/19

- and for me to be an easy target - but I suspect that began in utero as my parents were fighting back then.

Were my sleep issues caused by anxiety, or anxiety caused by sleep issues?

I just never liked anyone to be upset or angry around me - then I had to deal with the wrath, and **CLEAN UP THE MESS.**

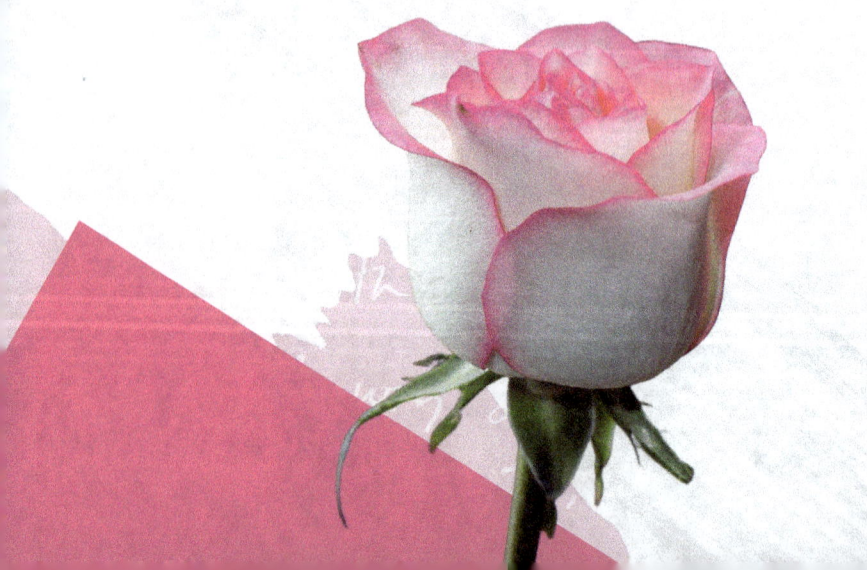

## 21.

I will never forget the day I was riding
in my Mom's truck. I was twenty-one
years old. I can't remember what we
were arguing about. She wanted me to
do something and I resisted.

And I had her **STOP THE CAR** so I could
get out.

We were close to home, but I had just
had it with her. I wonder if these
times - the way she didn't respect
my needs, wants, boundaries - was it
because she was troubled or because I
was an easy target?

I did have sleep issues all my life,
which caused me to have a lot of anxiety

er wanted was a quiet life, a simple life.
to write, do yoga - live by the water.
cancer - a water baby. My body is made o
I love to be in the water. I love to be by
water.
— I am the water. —

eeking, always trying to get unstuck.

fully giving myself permission to let go of w
safe and what I know.

nown, the uncomfortable too hard, scary, pa

Parliamo dei
fotografi di moda con
lavorato.
Penso che siano degli
Richard Avedon mi di
modella è come un'att
muto. Non ha a disposiz
dialogo ma dare esp
grafo l
el naso
ellezza
che ho
della.
divent
ice de
ggiung

38 cop
sta di
li Zho

già âgée po
sembravo mo
ane!

**OUR DEEPEST FEAR IS NOT THAT WE ARE INADEQUATE.**

Our deepest fear is that we are powerful beyond
measure. It is our light, not our darkness that
most frightens us.

We ask ourselves,

**'WHO AM I TO BE BRILLIANT, GORGEOUS, TALENTED,
FABULOUS?'**

Actually, who are you not to be?

**YOU ARE A CHILD OF GOD.**

Your playing small does not serve the world.
There is nothing enlightened about shrinking
so that other people won't feel insecure around
you.

**WE ARE ALL MEANT TO SHINE, AS CHILDREN DO.**

We're born to make manifest the glory of God
that is within us. It's not just in some of
us; it's in everyone. And as we let our own
light shine, we unconsciously give other people
permission to do the same. As we are liberated
from our own fear, our presence automatically
liberates others.

- Marianne Williamson

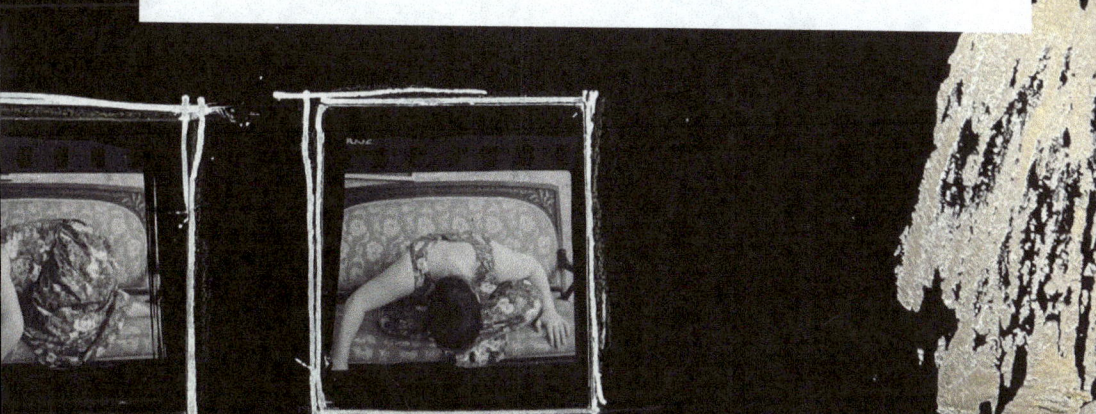

I deserve this. **I'M WORTH IT AND I BELIEVE IN MYSELF.**
Setting boundaries when there were none before,
and knowing I have a choice about it.

xo,
J

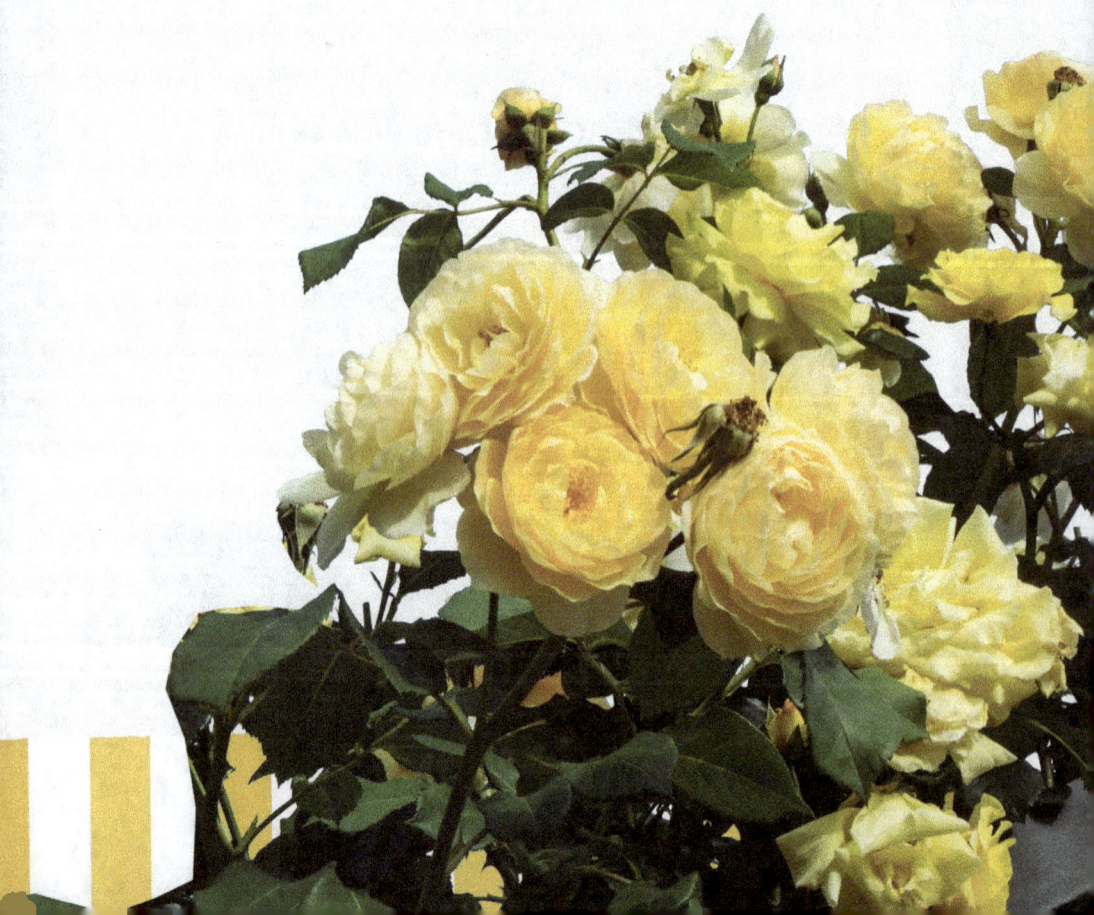

Dear Jenny,

My husband and I have come to Lake Crescent - near Port Angeles on the Olympic Peninsula. This lake is the most glorious, fresh water, be & peaceful place I know. Every summer we come her so I can float in the water and cleanse my soul.

I stand on the end of the dock — and say to myself "1, 2, 3 ... a Just do it!" The reward, in this case far outweighs the fear jumping in.

In a world where you are damned if you do and damned if you don't In a world where flying under the radar is not the safest bet - it's actually the most dangerous threat just jump. If you jump in the ring and shine too bright you are judged

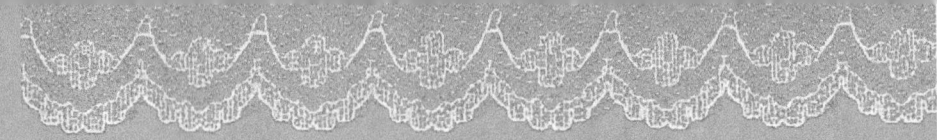

Dear Diary,

My Husband and I have come to Lake Crescent - near Port Angeles on the Olympic Peninsula.

This lake has the most glorious fresh water. It is the most beautiful and peaceful place I know. Every summer, we come here so I can f l o a t in the water and *cleanse my soul.*

I stand on the end of the dock and say to myself: "One, two, three…. Ah! Just do it!" And with that, suddenly I'm in the water. The reward in this case far outweighs the fear of jumping in.

In a world where you are:

**DAMNED IF YOU DO AND DAMNED IF YOU DON'T -**

In a world where flying under the radar is not the safest bet, it's actually the most dangerous threat - **JUST JUMP.** Just bet on yourself.

If you jump in the ring and shine too bright, you are judged.

You are judged if you fall down and fail, too.

If you don't go for your dreams, you are judged as well- so you might as well have fun.

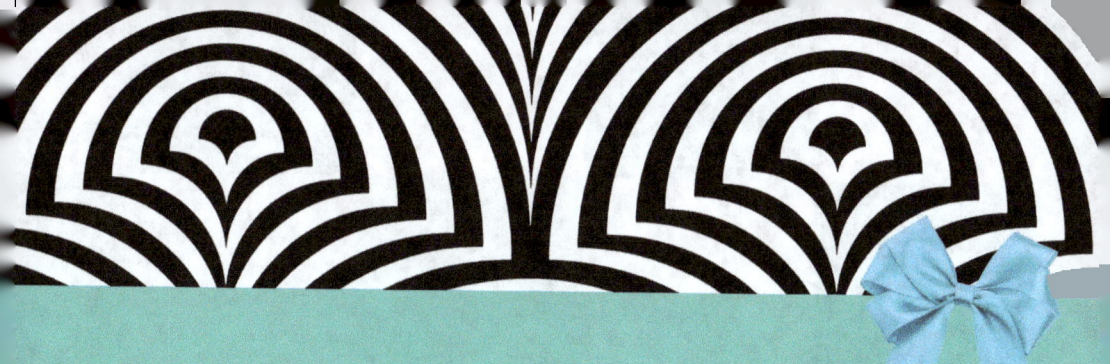

## 9/22/2022

I used to drive by dark houses with the blinds drawn shut, and think how sad it was for the lonely people who lived there.

**HOW SAD FOR THE LONELY, DARK HOUSE.**

Now I just drive by and think how happy those folks might be to have privacy and solitude.

How satisfying the life the house has led.

How full, bright, open, noisy, loved.

The house is having a well-deserved rest.

We all need a rest sometimes.

More often than not.

**ALL THE CRACKED PAINT, STAINS, BROKEN PATHWAYS, AND WEEDS - THEY ALL ADD UP TO A LIFE WELL LIVED, JUST LIKE THE PEOPLE LIVING THERE.**

# Part Two

*"The days are long but the years are short"*
-Gretchen Rubin

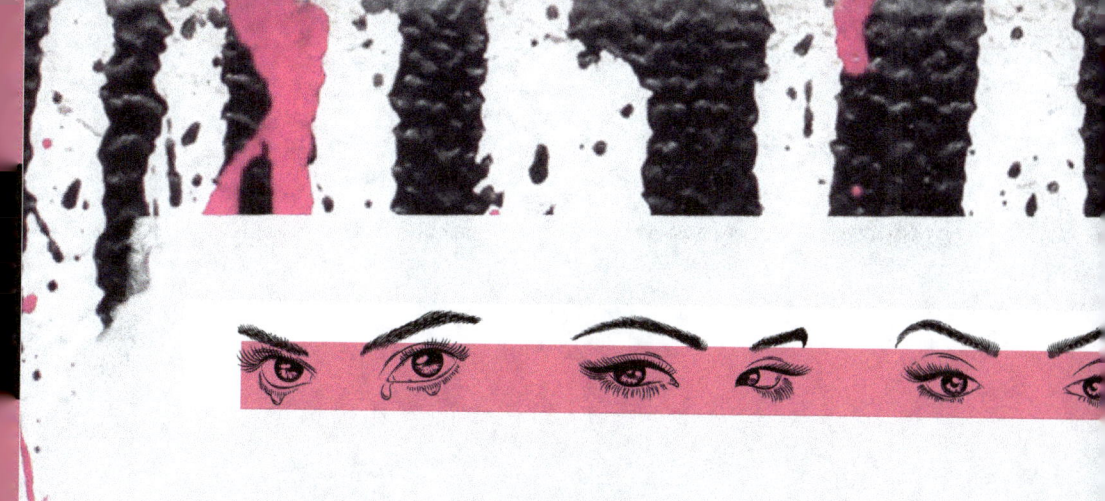

# EYES

If I am always looking at myself
through your eyes -
I will never see clearly.
Your vision is not mine.
The way you see yourself is so incorrect.
Trying to please -
while at the same time exerting a very strong,
clear independence. It's exhausting.
I guess I'm much more like you than not.

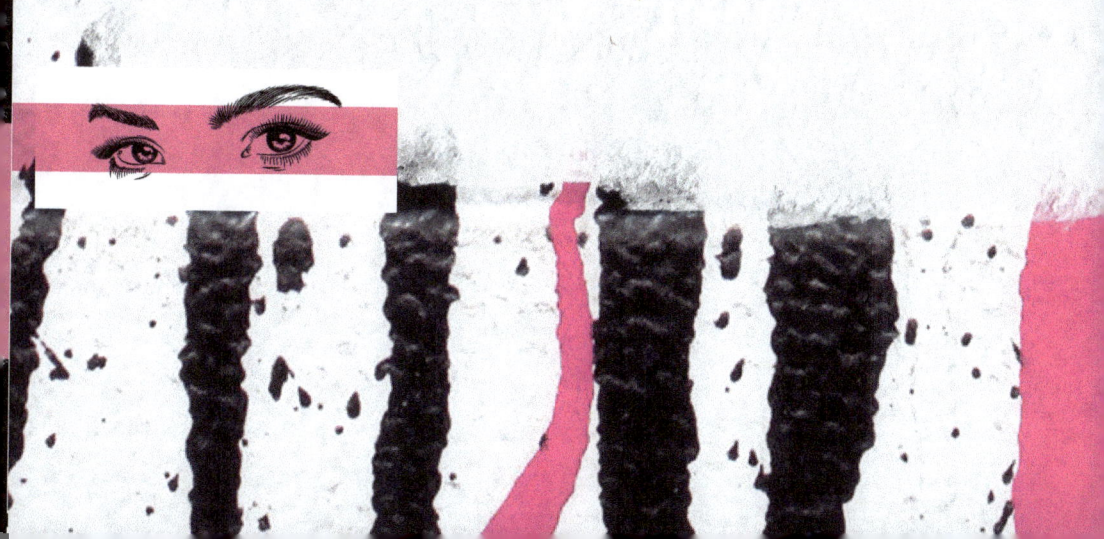

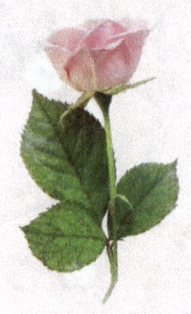

Is it that it's ok to go for your dreams, as long as they are chosen from this pre-approved list provided to you by family and society?

Life is truly short. He would have been 77 this year, my father. He passed away 11 years ago. Enjoy it, love the process, embrace the ups and downs- the toil, the sweat, the tears, the heartbreak.

**LOVE ALL OF IT - BECAUSE THAT'S WHAT MAKES US HUMAN.**

It is what makes it worth it. Never taking it for granted.

I would rather have a huge heartbreak because I took a chance than a low level fear coursing through my body at all times caused by the chances I didn't take. There will always be fear, so choose your fear.

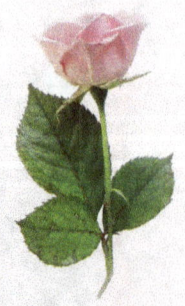

instead of being grateful for
what/how it already is.
— Venice is sinking.

RICCI

I learned my worth
[for it]
by stopping looking ^ from som
who would never be able to
give it to me — and looked
inside myself instead.

How did I get here? I hav
no idea — let's start with
where did I come from? Ho
far have I come? Where am
I going. You know, they say
there is no "there" there. But
I would say I'm like 40
```
```

- I used to drive
by dark houses
with the blinds
drawn shut, and
think how sad

it was for the lonely people who
lived there. How sad for the lonely,
dark house. Now I just drive by
and think how happy those folks
might be for privacy and solitude.
how satifying the life the house
has led. How full, bright, open,
noisy, loved. The house is
just having a rest. We all need
rest sometimes. More often than
not. All the cracked paint, stains,
broken pathway, weeds - they all
add up to a life well lived, just like

I wish I could match my insides to my outsides - or rather - my outsides to my insides. Most of all - the truth. The positive, bright, light, shining Truth. The truth is - the self-doubt, the negativity, the dark - is the lie. You make your own reality, you choose. Sometimes you have to dig down to the depths of the ocean that is your soul, and ask a higher power for that glimmer of truth - but I promise - if you do - you will find it there waiting for you. Here is to health, freedom, and creativity and a life full of truth. :)

I wish I could match my insides to my
outsides- or rather,

My outsides to my insides.

Most of all - tell the **TRUTH.**

The positive, bright, light, shining Truth.

The truth is - the self-doubt, the negativity,
the dark is the lie.

## YOU MAKE YOUR OWN REALITY.

You choose.

Sometimes you have to

dig
down
to the depths
of the ocean
that is
your soul,

and ask a higher power for the truth.

But I promise, if you do - you will find it
there waiting for you.

Here is to health, freedom, and creativity -
and a life lived in absolute truth. - J.

Venice, Italy

Dear Love,

- Did you get the Love
that you needed? Where do
it come from? Maybe the
Suffering exists in the looki
for it outside. Maybe its al
the Love that you give. Mayb
all those rejections, teflon
projections weren't about you

## Dear Love,

Did you get the love that you needed?

Where does it come from?

Maybe the suffering exists in looking for it outside.

Maybe it's about the Love that you give.

Maybe all those rejections, **teflon projections** weren't about you, they were about them.

Maybe the suffering is in the wanting everything to be different, instead of being grateful for what and how it already is.

I learned my worth when I stopped looking for it from someone who would never be able to give it to me -

and looked inside myself instead.

## HOW DID I GET HERE?

I have no idea

let's start with

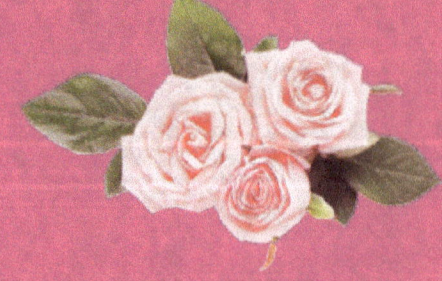

## WHERE DID I COME FROM?
## WHERE AM I GOING?

You know, they say there is no "there" there.

Tearing down one of many walls, one wall at a time.

I'm still learning.

I will always be learning.

I'm just exhausted from all this construction.

Dear Diary,

I thought I had figured it all out. I thought I was done. After ending communication with my mom - I thought I was all fixed, and totally free.

What I'm realizing is that I'm not done, and I'm <u>not</u> completely free. I still am a bit stuck - feeling that I don't deserve to live my dreams. I think I'm still self-sabotaging, or letting FEAR rule my decisions. I am on a journey to sever ties with my inner asshole, and replace that voice with the Truth of who I am. I am going back to Therapy. This will be a lifelong journey - but

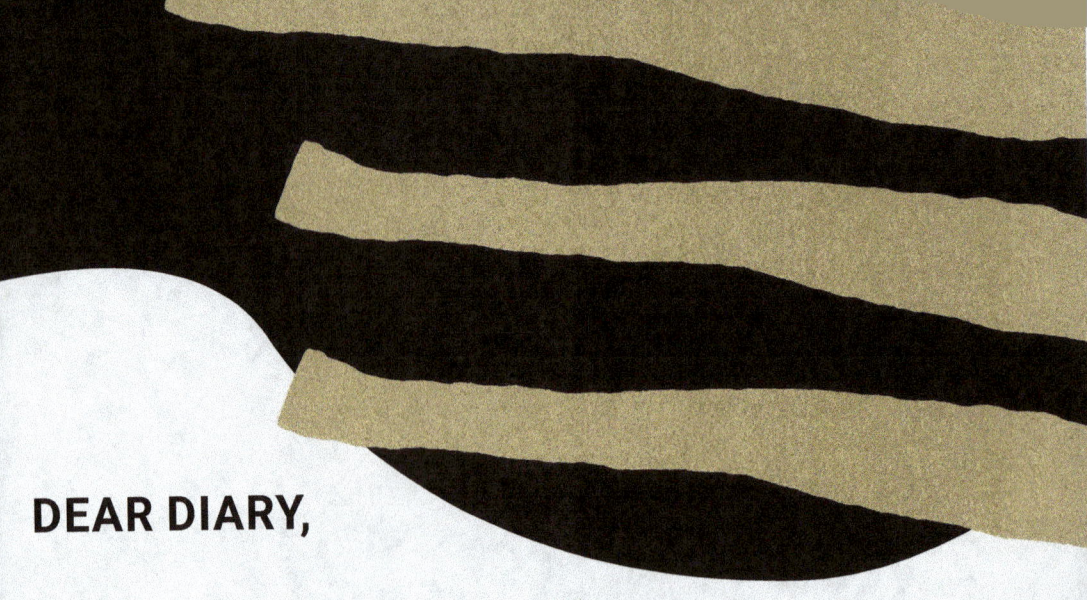

## DEAR DIARY,

I thought I had figured it all out.

I thought I was done.

After ending communication with my Mom - I thought I was all fixed, and totally free.

What I am realising is that I am not done, and I am not completely free.

I still am a bit stuck - feeling that I don't deserve to live my dreams.

I think I'm still self-sabotaging, or letting FEAR rule my decisions.

I am on a journey to sever ties with my inner asshole and replace that *voice* with the *truth* of who I am.

I am going back to therapy.

This will be a lifelong journey - but all I want is to set myself free.

~As Elizabeth Gilbert says:

"There is no such thing as one way liberation."

xo J.

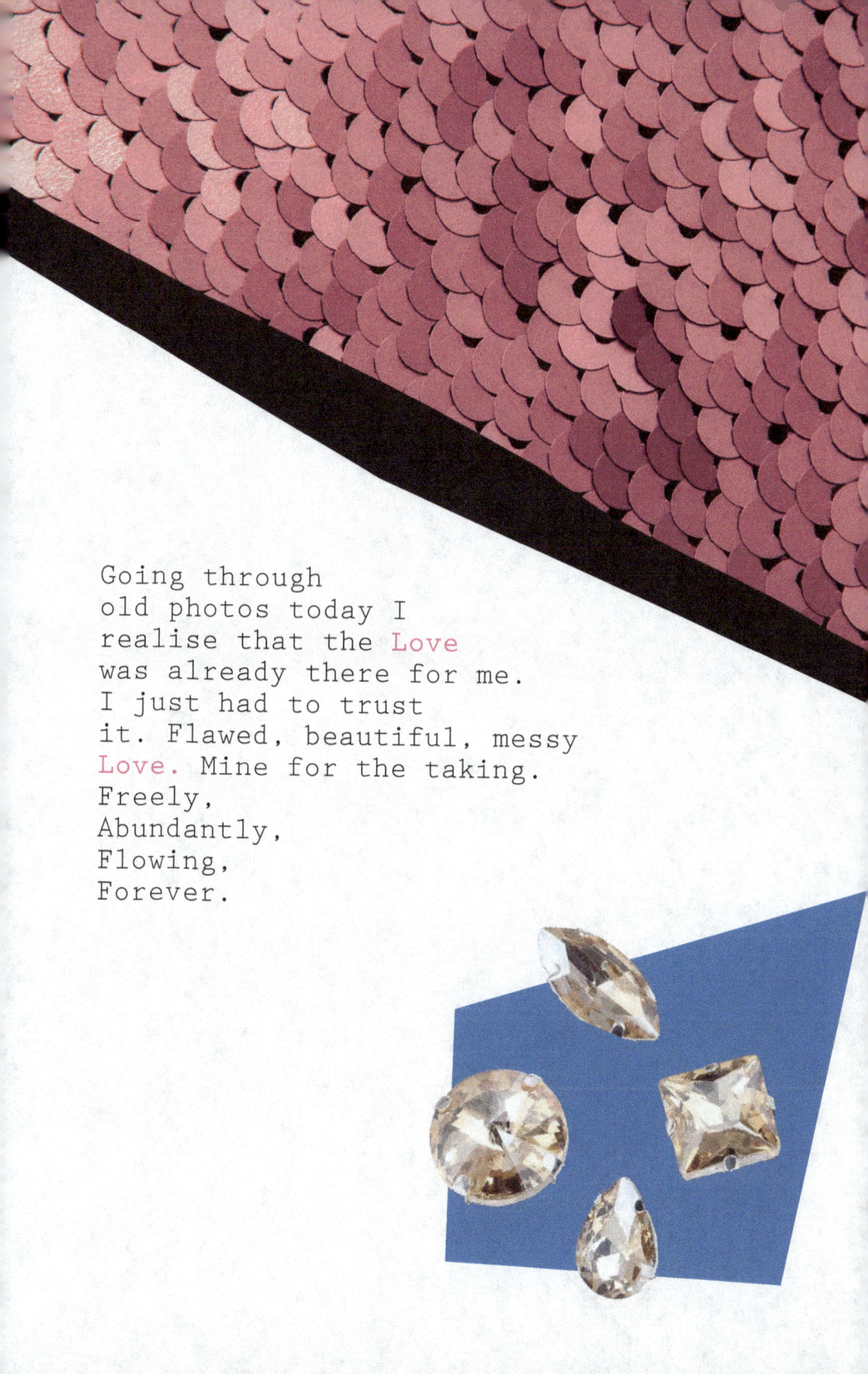

Going through
old photos today I
realise that the Love
was already there for me.
I just had to trust
it. Flawed, beautiful, messy
Love. Mine for the taking.
Freely,
Abundantly,
Flowing,
Forever.

e Mother, one Father - one boy
ne girl. I think my family
as trying to be something it
wasn't - Pretending to be perfect.
This caused quite a bit of suffering.
Truth is - I had one dad, two moms,
one brother - etc.... How fortunate
was I?

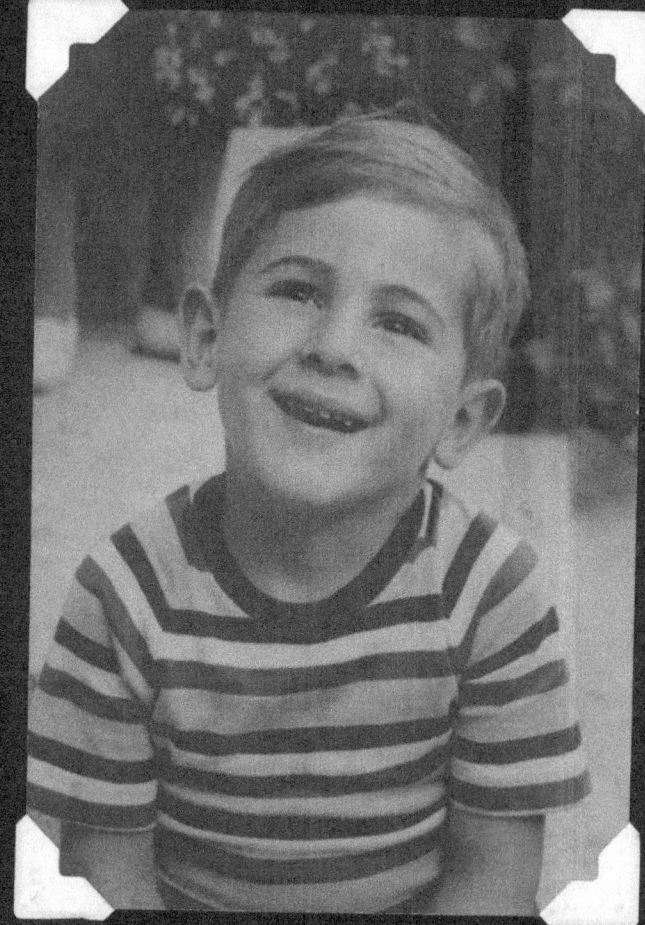

My Father — Remi Ricci - (Age 4)
— Hat boro, PA

# What makes a family?

Is it one Mother, one Father - one boy, one girl?

It could be anything.

What you choose, what you have, what you create.

I think my family was trying to be something it wasn't - pretending to be perfect.

This caused quite a bit of suffering.

Truth is-
I had one Dad,
two Moms,
one Brother,
two Brothers…

*How fortunate was I?*

# DEAR LOVE,

Let go, let go of what no longer belongs to me.

Or what never did belong to me.

Let go of what I was told I wanted.

All those years of being told:
you don't have needs, wants, dreams, or desires.

How dare you!
All those years of the world slapping my hand and
saying "No! This is not for you!"

*These dreams.*

**YOU ARE HERE TO COMPLY, BE QUIET, SMALL,
ACCOMMODATING, SELFLESS, SERVE.**

I don't want to hold on to what wasn't mine to
begin with out of fear.

*I want to let go.*

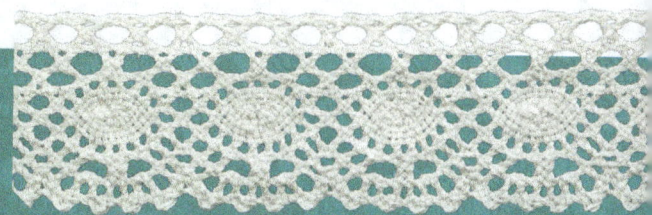

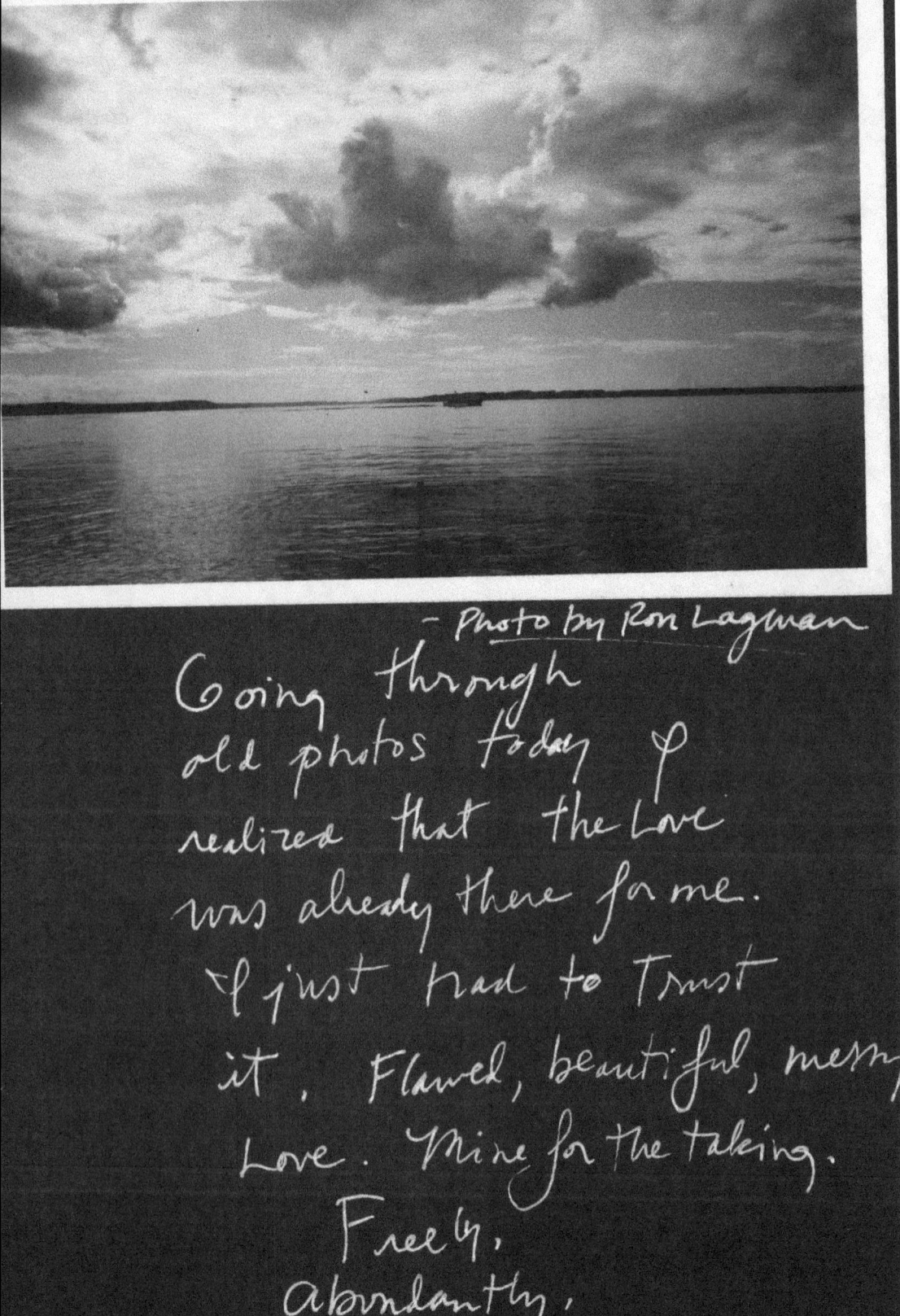

— Photo by Ron Lagman

Going through
old photos today I
realized that the Love
was already there for me.
I just had to Trust
it. Flawed, beautiful, messy
Love. Mine for the taking.
Freely,
Abundantly,
flowing,

- months - or advertisements that somehow creep under your skin without you noticing.

To be clear - this isn't about Staff - It's about people, animals, location, occupation, anything and everything.

It is up to you to define your life and listen to your heart. No one is up for that honorary task but you

XO
🖋

*what pulls me - all day long.*

*You will constantly hear such favorites as -*

*"I don't want that."*

Pilsen, Chicago 2000

Or "You will Love this!" coming from various opinion-stuffed olives (and olive stuffed mouths).

Or advertisements that somehow creep under your skin without you noticing.

To be clear: this isn't about stuff- it's about people, pets, location, occupation, anything and everything.

It is up to you to define your life and listen to your heart.

No one is up for that honorary task but you. XO, J.

"I guess that's what Mary Olive meant when she said "You o have to let the soft animal o your body love what it loves.

I guess that's what Mary Oliver meant when she said: "You only have to let the soft animal of your body love what it loves."

I think I'm finally beginning to understand why I got this tattooed on my arm. Now it's all making sense.

It truly isn't a matter of "I will only be happy when…"

It truly is a daily, active ritual of "What do I Love," along with a little "What do I need?" and a lot of "What do I desire?"

Ask yourself that every morning. What pulls me all day long? What is that little voice inside of me whispering?"

You will constantly hear such favourites in response: "You don't want that."

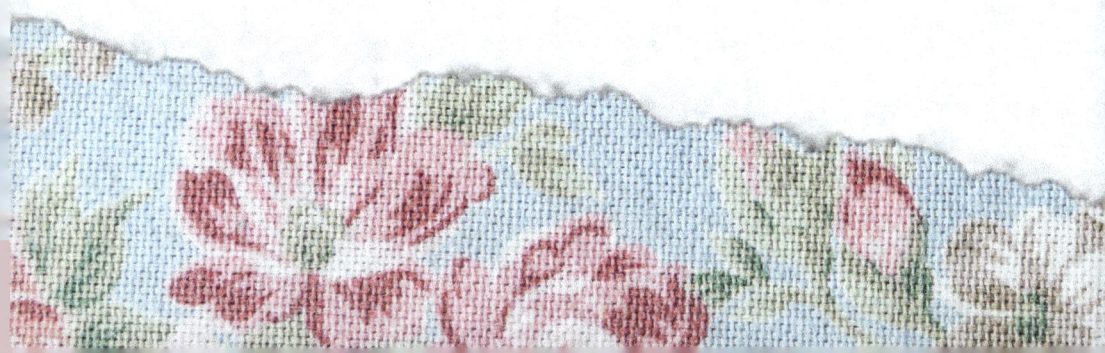

Dear Love,

Let go, let go of what no longer belongs to me. Or what never did belong to me. Let go, of what I was told I wanted. All those years of being told - you don't have needs, or wants, or desires, or dreams. How dare you - all those years, of the world slapping my hand saying "NO! This is not for you." This = dream: you are here to comply. Be quiet, small, accomodating, self-less, serve. I don't want to hold on to what wasn't mine to begin with out of fear.

One night I reached up,
pulled the Universe towards me and
whispered quietly in its ear:

*"I'm done messing around - Let's do
this!"*

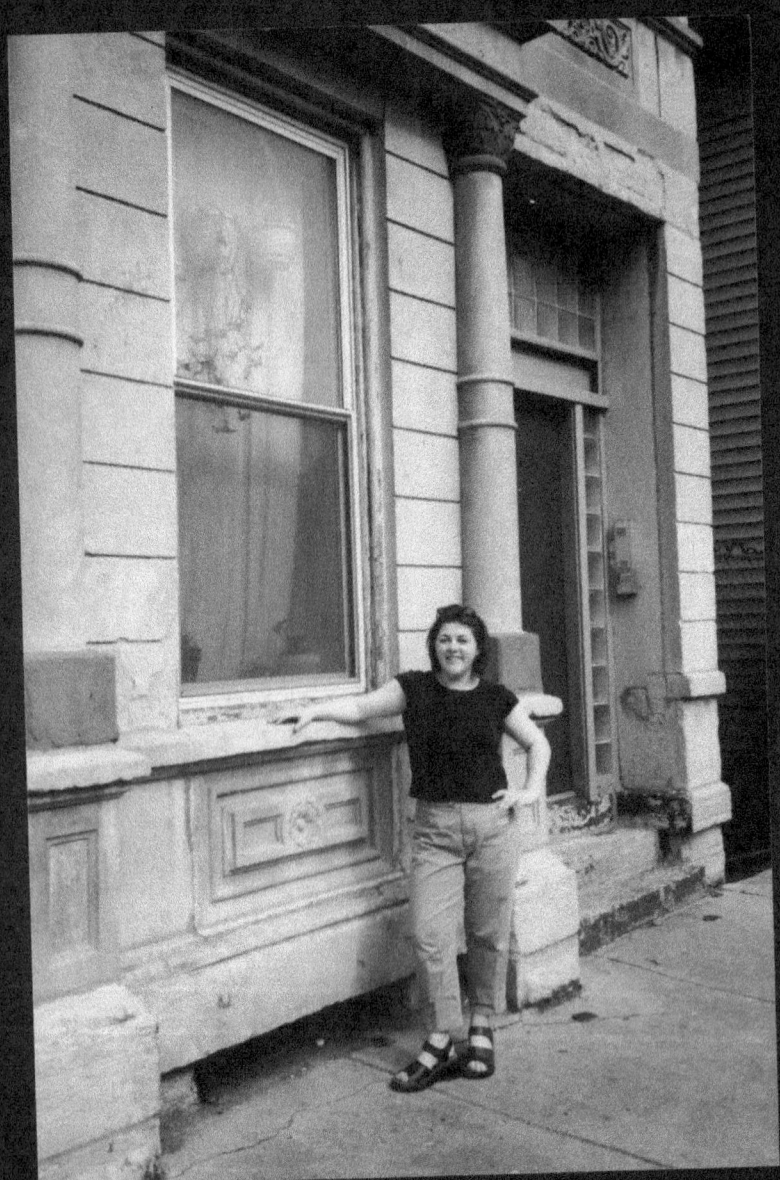

Pilsen, Chicago 2001

limitless ...

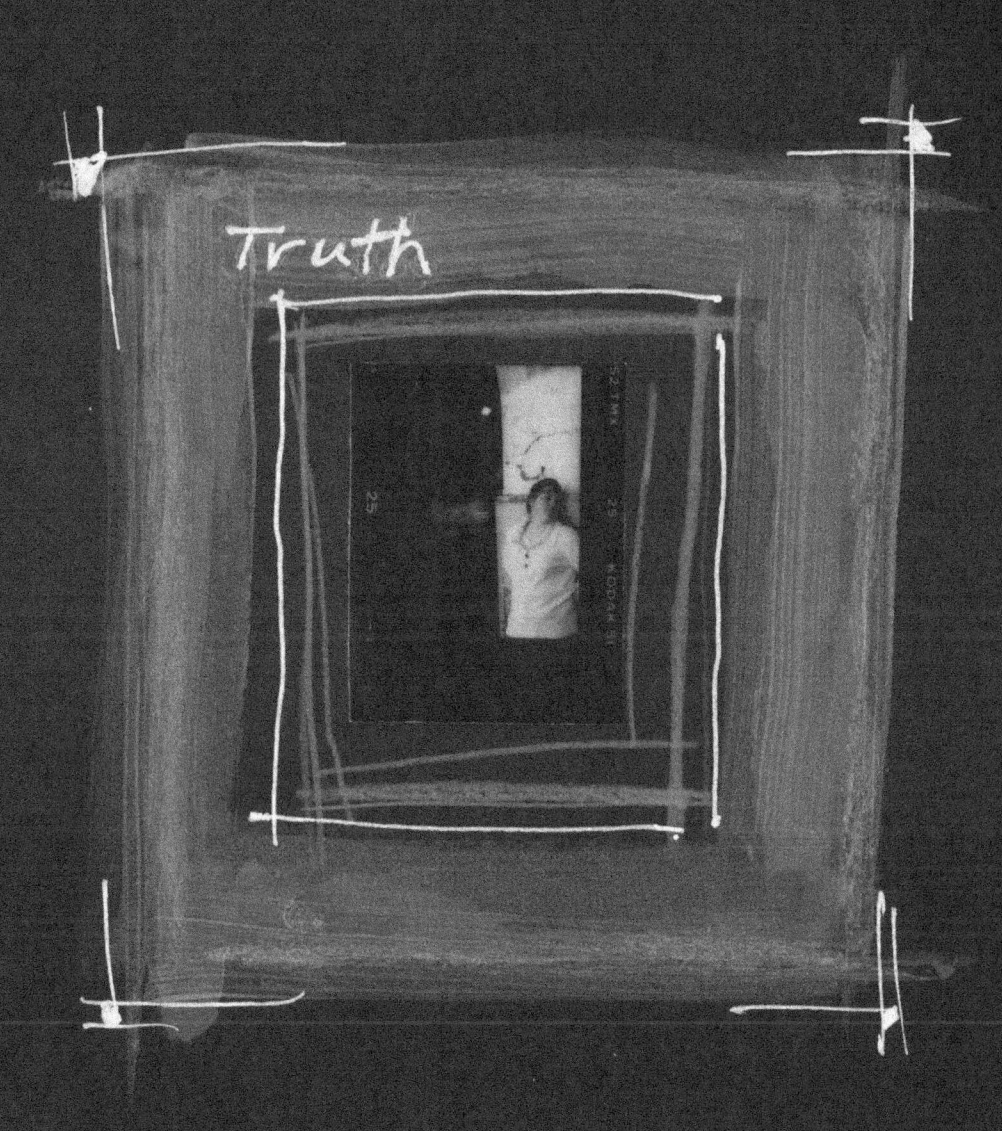

# Tenderness

Oh, tender heart. Don't
be so hard on yourself.
Please realize that none
of this is real.    What is real
is that you are amazing  and
lovely  and the world is at
your feet,  not against you.

Stop wasting your time
worrying about  who your
enemy is today - and embrace
all the Love in your life.
Don't forget to include yourself
in that circle.

Don't forget to dance when

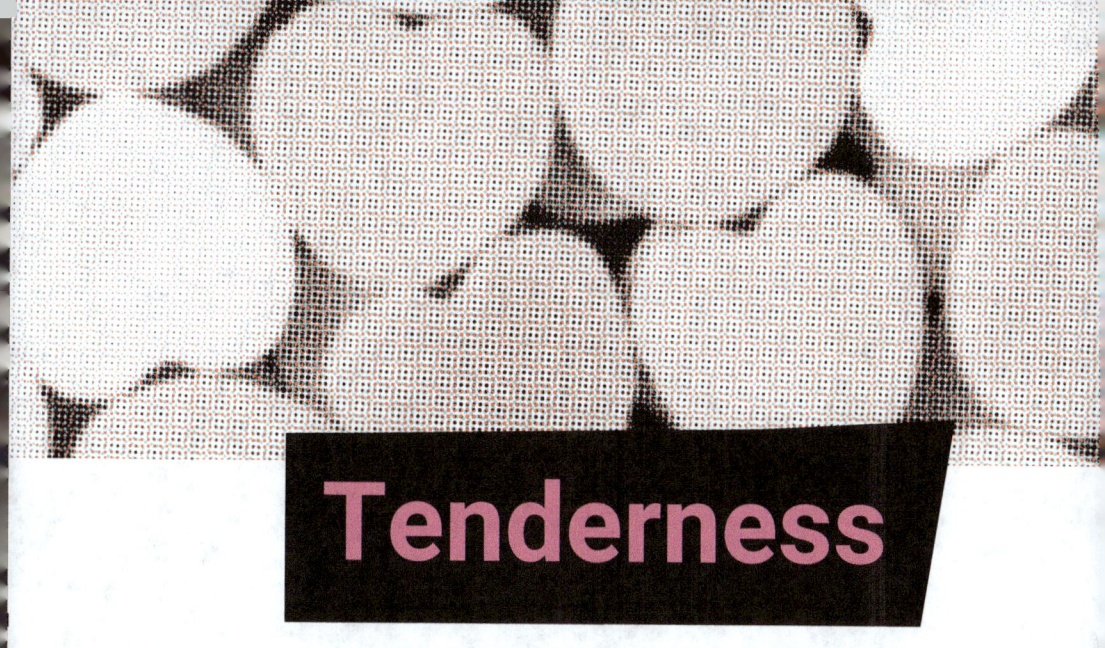

# Tenderness

Oh, tender heart. Don't be so hard on yourself.
Please realise that none of this is real.

What is real is that you are amazing and lovely
and the world is at your feet, not against you as
it may seem to be the case.

Stop wasting your time worrying about who your
enemy is today and embrace all the Love in your
life. You are not in a war zone, even though
it may feel that way. Don't forget to include
yourself in that circle of **LOVE.**

Don't forget to dance when you are supposed to be
working. Fuck it.  Life is truly too short. You
have a gift. Sharing it is the best thing that you
can do to move the world in the right direction.

xo J.

One night I reached up,
Pulled the Universe
towards me -
and whispered quietly in its
ear:

"I'm done messing around-
Let's do this!"

**I** finally understand that they may have been wrong. I guess that's why I was so lost and confused.

By they I mean family, society, the news, the mainstream view found - rather, hammered upon us daily.

Constantly whispering in our ear, sneaking under our skin, sneaking in the back door.

So much so that we become numb to it. And so so tired from running around trying to please all these voices.

I decided to take a delicious nap and go on a journey to find my voice. The only one that matters.

Yours is the only one who knows what is right for you, **AND THE ONLY ONE THAT IS TRUE.**

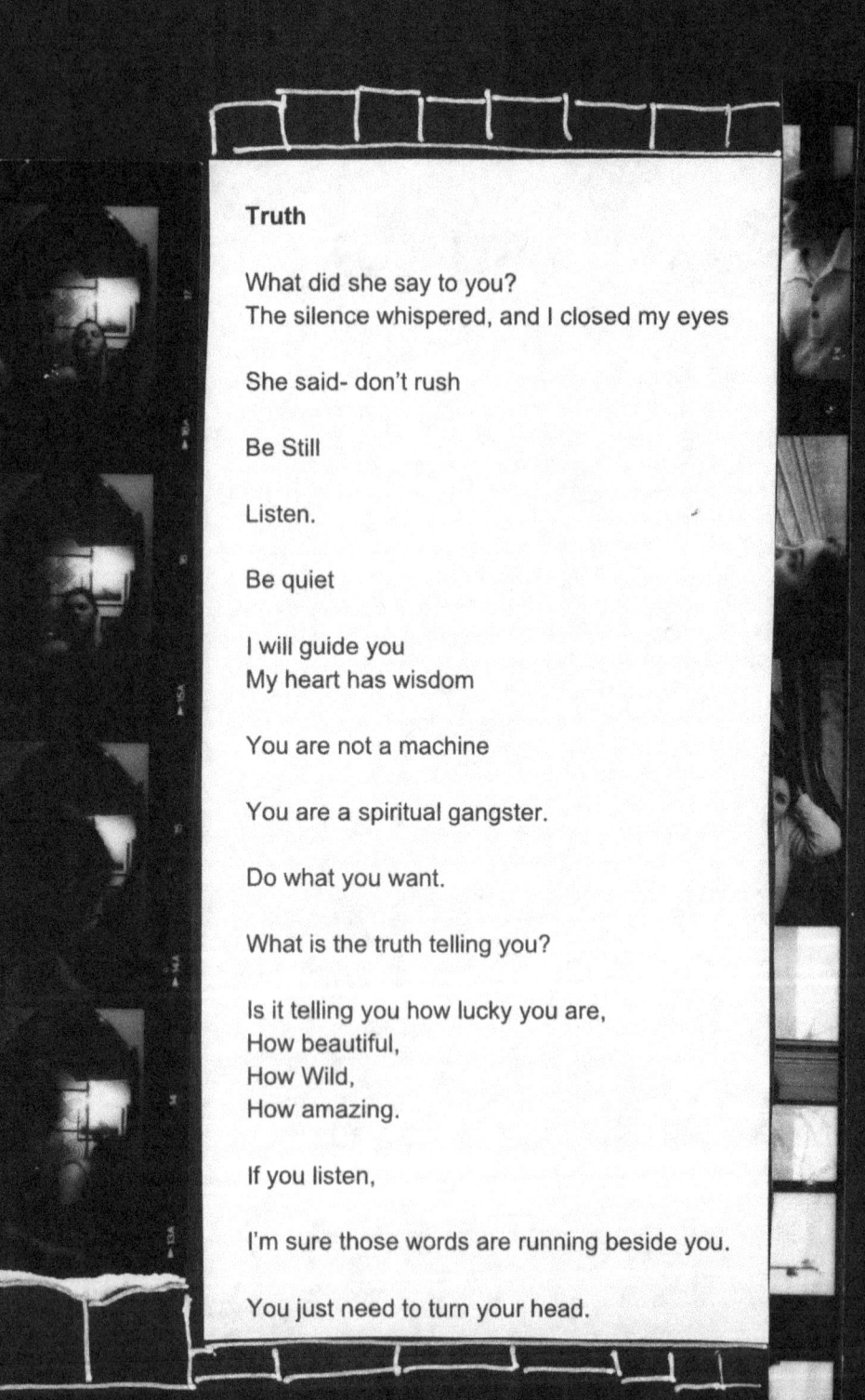

### Truth

What did she say to you?
The silence whispered, and I closed my eyes

She said- don't rush

Be Still

Listen.

Be quiet

I will guide you
My heart has wisdom

You are not a machine

You are a spiritual gangster.

Do what you want.

What is the truth telling you?

Is it telling you how lucky you are,
How beautiful,
How Wild,
How amazing.

If you listen,

I'm sure those words are running beside you.

You just need to turn your head.

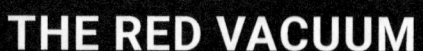

# THE RED VACUUM

I'm 41. I take my Mom to the clinic to get her
blood pressure checked. It is still too high for
her to have eye surgery. My Mom turns and says to
me as we are leaving the clinic

"Will you go with me to Europe?"

She wants me to go because she can't see.

I don't react well - What about your health? I
think to myself. Let's deal with that first? Here
we are- trying to figure out what to do about her
eyes - and she wants to talk about Europe. When we
arrive at her house, we talk about calling another
doctor.

"Mom, what do you want to do?"  I ask.

She becomes fixated on a little red vacuum that
I left at her house when we lived there. She
starts attempting to vacuum the floor, with very
little success.  It doesn't work.  She asks why I
don't take it with me. I get so upset with her -
obsessed with the vacuum, and not facing the hard

It's hard to believe that people could really Love me.

I am nothing, or so I feel  It's hard to believe, when you come home to so much that is unpredictable.

It is even harder when you spend your life wanting for things to be different than they are.

And for not loving what you already have.

-Juliette

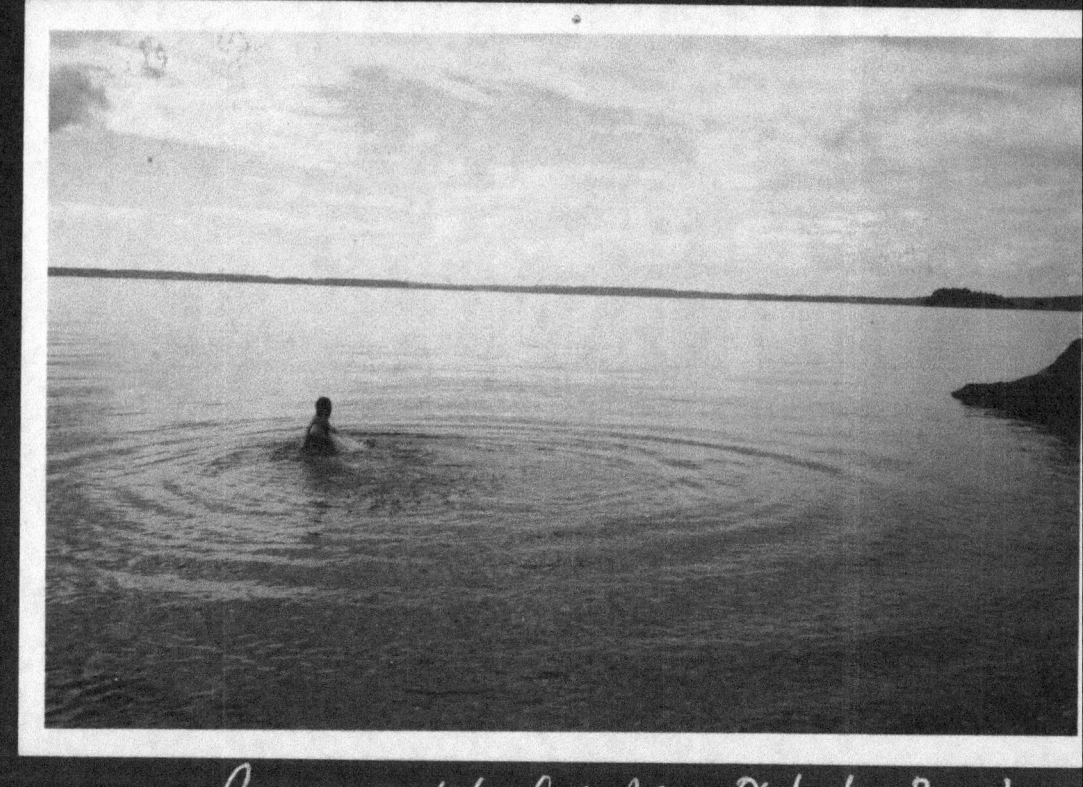

Camano Island, WA · Photo by Ron Layu

I finally understand that they
may have been wrong. I guess that's
why I was so lost and confused.
By they I mean family, friends,
society, the news, the mistaken
views found - no, hammered
upon us daily. So much so
that we become numb to it,
and so so tired from running
around trying to please
all these voices.

I decided to take a delicious
nap - and go on a journey for
my voice. The only one that
matters. Yours is the only one
who knows what is right for
you, and the only one that is
true.

I am 41, I take my mom to the clinic to get her blood pressure checked. It is still too high to have eye surgery. Mom says to me as we leave the clinic "will you go with me to Europe?" She wants me to go because she can't see. I don't react well—Here we are, trying to figure out what to do about her eyes—and she wants to talk about Europe. When we get to her house we talk about calling another doctor. "mom, what do you want to do?" I ask. She becomes fixated on a little red vacume that I left at her house. She tries to use it—it doesn't work. She asks why I don't take it with me. I get so upset after her obsession w/ it—not facing the hard decisions of her health. I truly don't care if she gets the surgery, I'm just here to help. But she can't help herself. I finally agree to take the damn vacume leave in a huff and throw it under the porch. I just can't put it in my car I just can't do it anymore.

decisions about the health of her eyes.
I don't care if she gets the surgery, I am just
there to help. I don't want her to blame me for
missing an opportunity, and I really resent her
wasting my time.

But she can't help herself. I finally agreed to
take the damn vacuum. I leave in a huff and throw
it under the porch. I just can't seem to make
myself put the broken red vacuum in my car. I just
can't do it anymore. I just can't do one more
thing she asks me to do when I don't want to.

I don't want to because I feel that this broken
red Dirt Devil symbolises all the things she
cared about more than me, and herself, and is a
distraction from what I was there to do.

Yet another example of me being less important
than anything and everything else in her life.

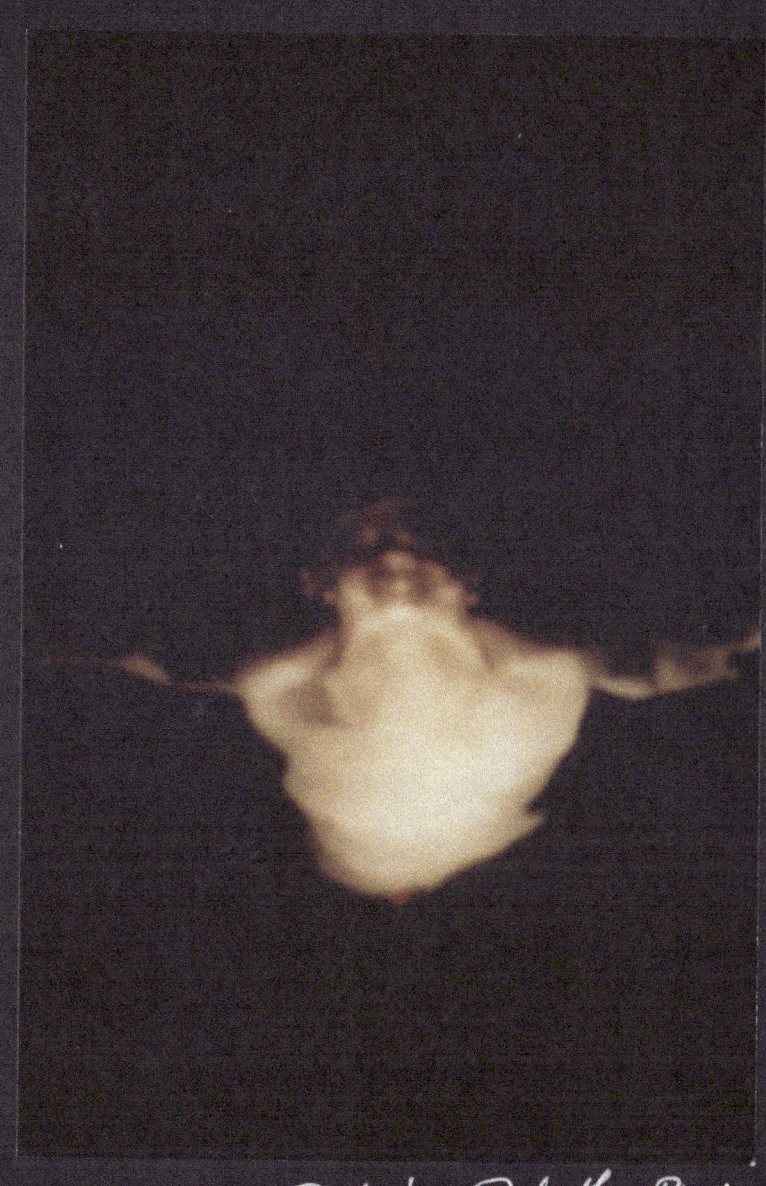

Photo by Juliette Ricci

like scrambled eggs to you, dear reader? This is what it's like in my brain. I hope it can be appreciated. I truly want to provide a clean picture. Scrambled eggs. A clean picture of my childhood.

---

At age 40 I started heavy therapy after we moved in with my mom - as she was embarking on a ten month trip to Europe. We were "house-sitting." Part of coming to moms was trying to understand why she was the way she was. Why was she so mean to me? Why everytime I spoke to her - she could tear me to shreds with very few words (sometimes with just one word).

That's all it took.

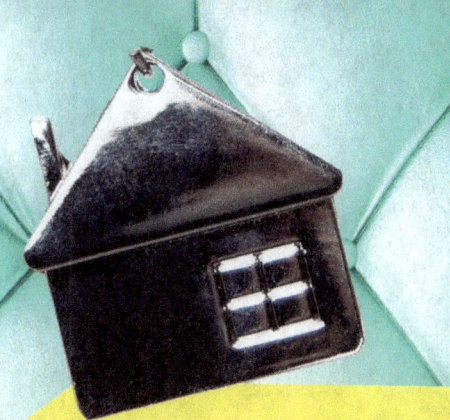

Scrambled eggs?
Does this all seem like scrambled eggs to you, dear reader?
This is what it's like in my brain.
I hope it will be appreciated.
I truly want to provide a clear picture.
Scrambled eggs.
They are how I order them every time.

At age 40, I started heavy therapy after we moved in with my Mom. She was about to embark on a 10 month trip to Europe.

We were 'house sitting.'

Part of coming to mom's was trying to understand why she was the way she was.

Why was she so mean to me? Why everytime I spoke to her, she could tear me to shreds with very few words.

Sometimes all it took was one single word to slay me. Why do I put my whole self worth in other people's hands, only to be crushed time and time again?

One word. All it took was one word.

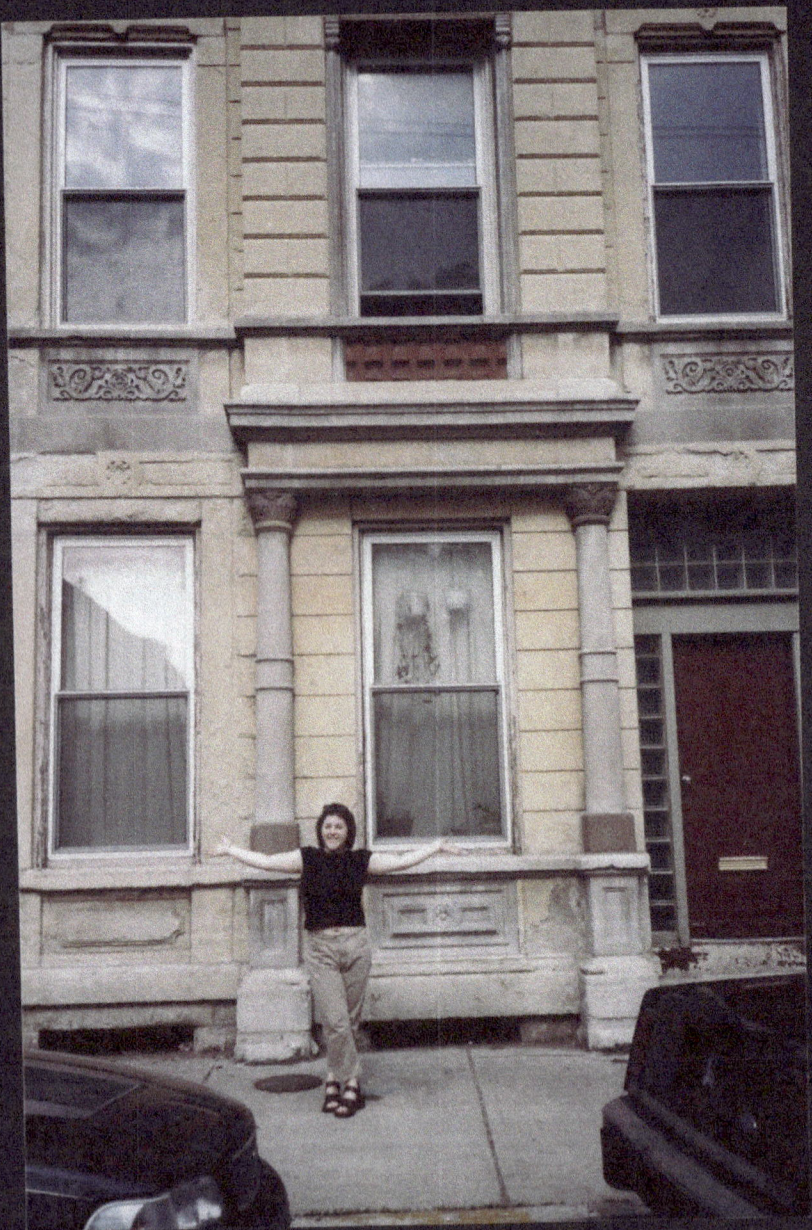

Pilsen, Chicago 2001

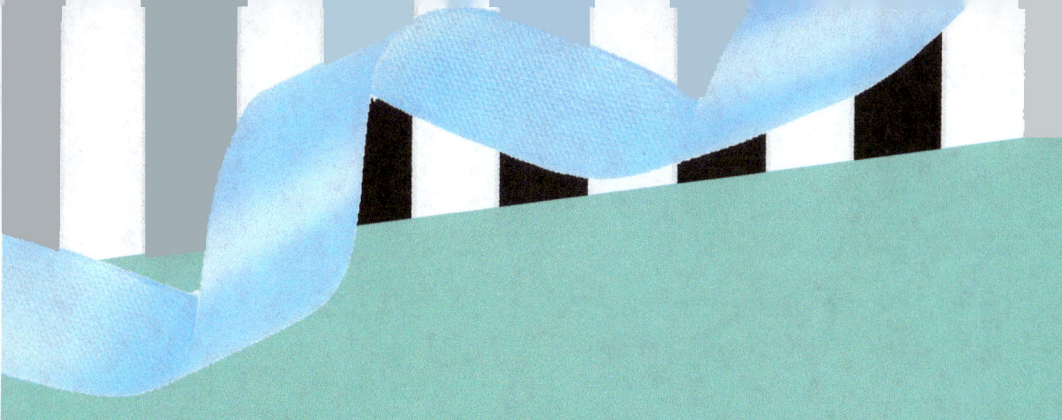

## <u>MASSA LUBRENSE, ITALY - OCTOBER 2023</u>

The water was so warm and salty - when I crept in, slowly.

It welcomed me.

As I floated and tread water - and waved my nails around caressing the water.

It was so amazing - I felt that I belonged there and that I was never meant to touch dry land again.

I felt one with the water.

My body - cradled - feeling so safe and embraced by love and truth.

I am the ocean.

It is undeniable.

**P.S.-**

In talking with my therapist lately I've realised
that I don't talk to her because i'm afraid i'm not
strong enough to handle her. She could say one
syllable, and crush me. Why does she think it's
ok to speak to me that way? I was always groomed
to make sure everyone around me was happy and
never spoke up if I was upset. Maybe it was a
defense mechanism for survival.
I just crumbled with one word from her. I don't
want to be a bad daughter so I just do what she
says to avoid a very uncomfortable tantrum and
her telling me I'm selfish or a bad person in
some form. I was being manipulated. I wish I
could learn to set boundaries, and to manage the
feelings that come up when she opens her mouth.
Watching her has taught me that I don't want to
make people feel that way. Specifically, to feel
bad about themselves after an interaction.
I'm letting myself feel the negative. By the
way, what about toxic positivity? Was I always
taught mind over matter (we grew up in Christian
Science), or to be positive about everything?
More likely I did that to myself so I could get
through the day and create the calm environment I
was thirsty for.

I am learning there is more to this story than
I once thought. I'd like to learn to take
responsibility for my life and get comfortable
with the darkness and the light. I'd like to
forgive. Forgive myself, forgive her - and set
myself free.

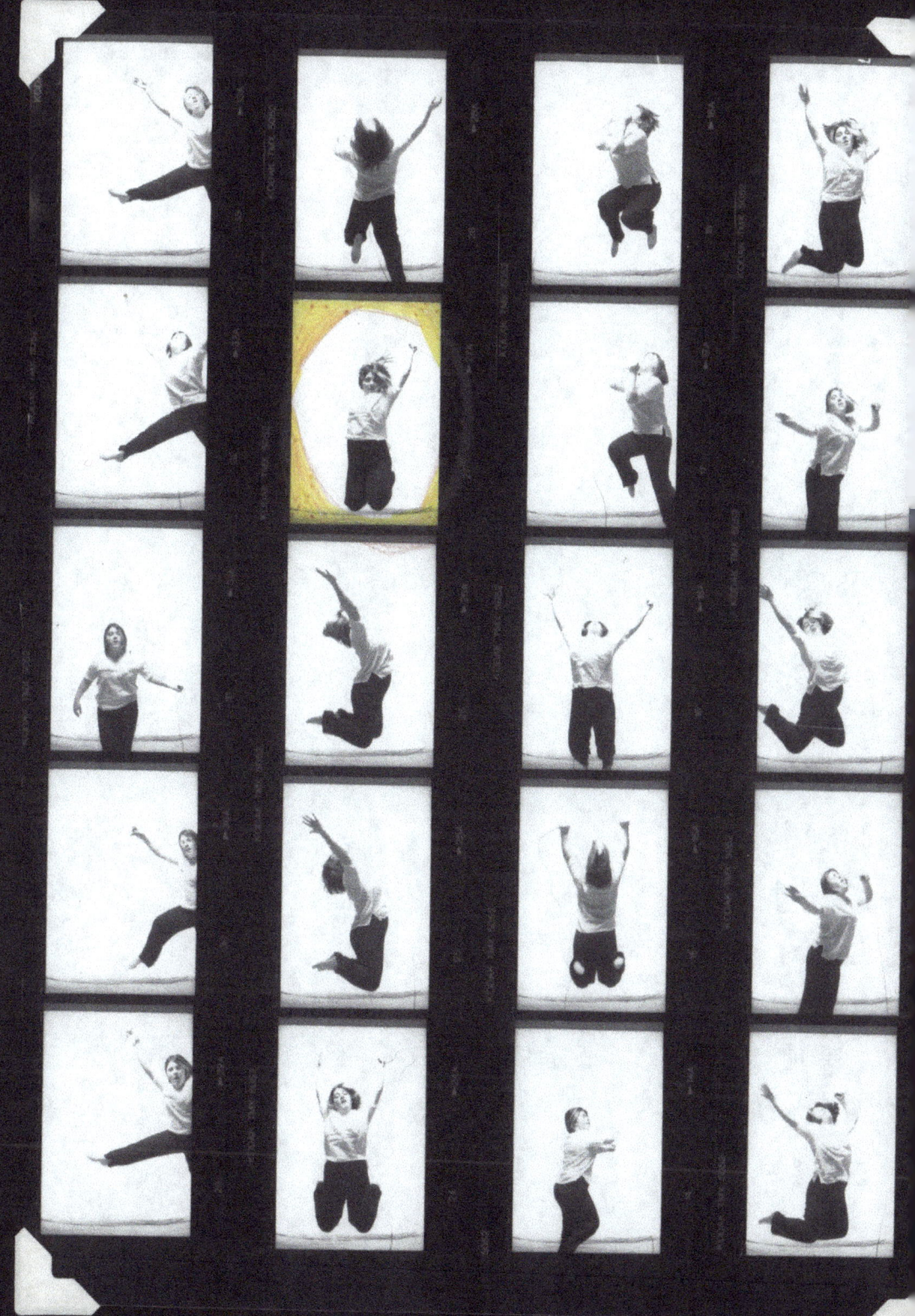

Self portraits - 1990 - EvCC

let's get on the road early!
don't forget to check those tires.

---

## - Tickets -

When I asked my HR Lady
about taking time off to travel -
her response was "Isn't
everything a once in a lifetime
opportunity" - I answered with
a big fat yes! This is after I
explained away "The once in a lifeti...
trip I was about to go on.

---

Stop wishing - buy the damn
ticket - and if you have a
ticket - cash it in.

---

## TICKETS

When I asked my HR lady about taking time off to travel -

I said "It's a once in a lifetime opportunity," her answer was:

"Isn't everything a once in a lifetime opportunity?" -

I answered with a big YES!

"The once in a lifetime trip" that I was about to embark on.

I will make memories that will last forever.

Stop wishing.

Buy the damn ticket and if you have a ticket-

Cash it in.

Mama Lubrenze, Italy October 2023

The water was so warm and
salty - when I crept in, slowly.

It welcomed me. As I floated,
and tread water - and waved
my nails around between the water.

It was so amazing - I never
wanted to leave. Perfect in its
warmth, beauty and sweet
rhythm. I felt as if I belonged
there, and never wanted to touch
dry land again. My body, cradled
- feeling so safe and embraced
by love and truth.

I feel I am the ocean.

XB, I.

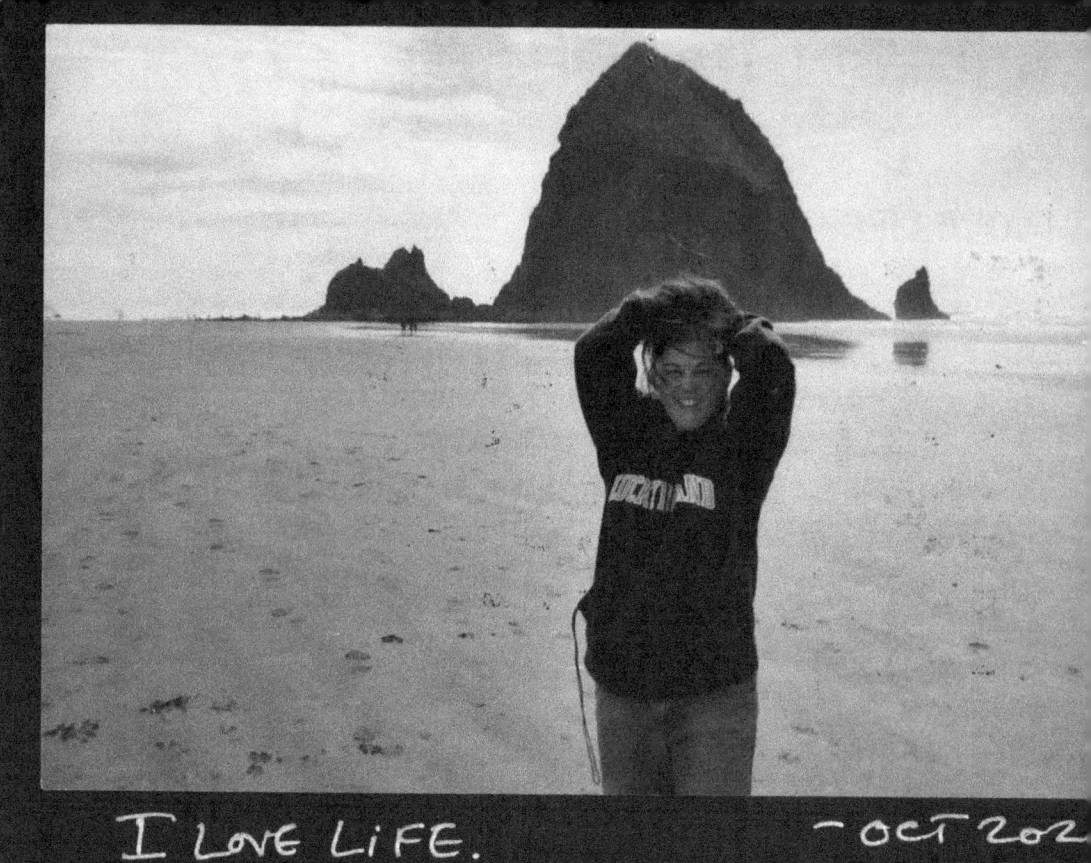

I LOVE LIFE.                    - OCT 2O2

You are not supposed to love yoursee
that much.    On this trip I realized
that I am alive . I was hoping for a
"hot girl fall" - getting my braces off
soon.   But now I am hoping for
just a hot girl life.   I was never
allowed to 'feel myself' - as I was sca
to shine - scared to love myself.  E
time I did I was shamed, put down,

## I LOVE LIFE - OCT 2023

You are not supposed to love yourself that much. On this trip I realised that I am, in fact, alive. I was hoping to have a 'hot girl fall' getting my braces off soon.

But now I'm hoping for just a hot girl life. I was never allowed to 'feel myself' - as I was scared to shine - scared to love myself.

Every time I did, I was shamed, put down, ridiculed. Maybe there was jealousy, or an element of 'stay in your lane' - so I can control and easily identify you.

## SO I CAN PREDICT WHAT YOU WILL DO NEXT AND BE COMFORTABLE WITH WHO YOU ARE.

I remember one time my mom said "you have guts" - her way of saying I was brave. And my brother said I was bold.

I want to embrace who I am. We all have dualities that co-exist.

Whatever the reason- I **AM** alive and I want to **BE** alive while I'm alive.

xo
J.

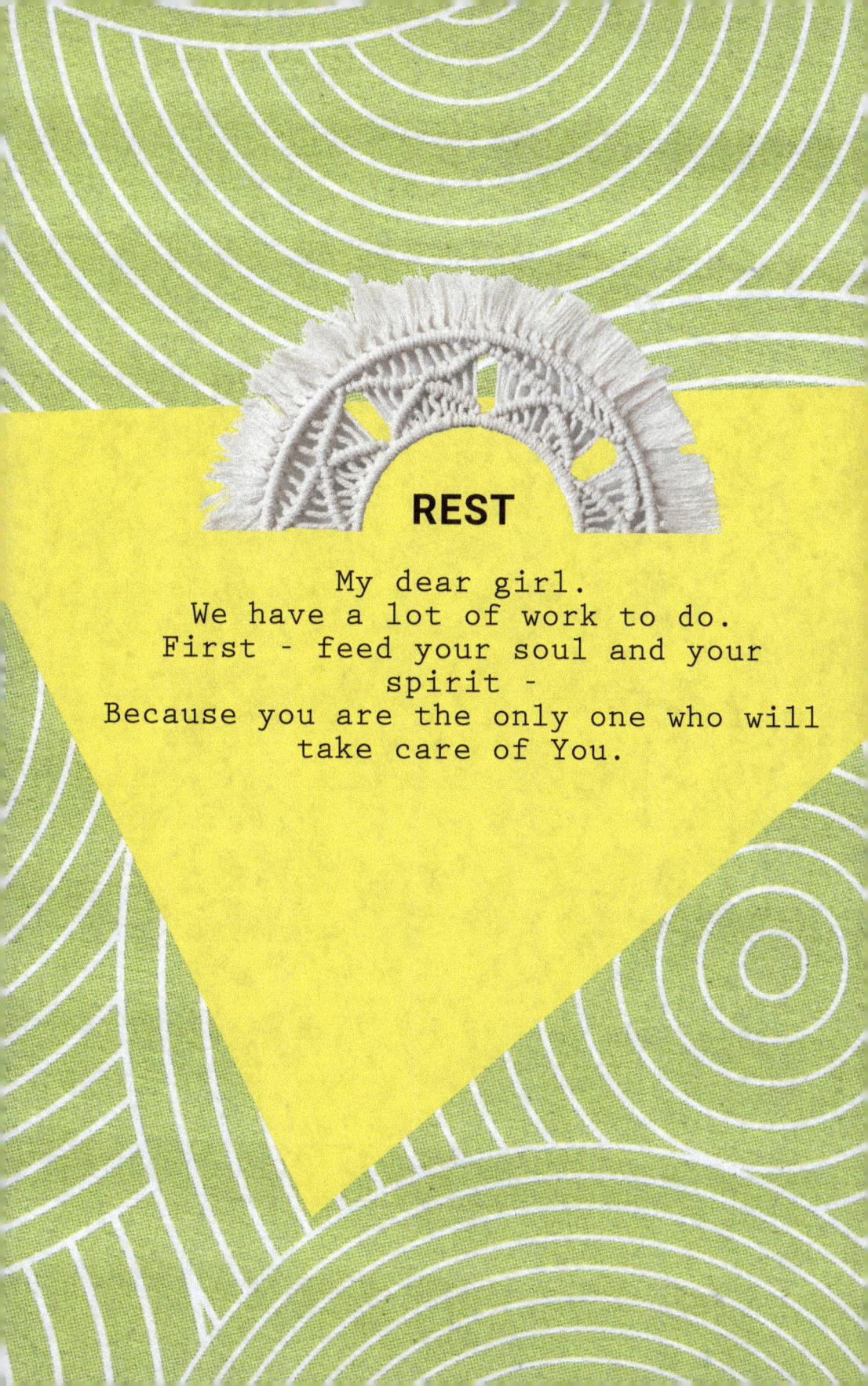

## REST

My dear girl.
We have a lot of work to do.
First - feed your soul and your
spirit -
Because you are the only one who will
take care of You.

Every morning I wake up and take a little blue pill. It's a numbing pill- a pill to help take the edge off my anxiety as I move throughout this world. Why do we feel the need to numb ourselves - what is wrong with our country, the world we live in that makes this a necessity to survive?

I'm going to start believing that I can ask for what I desire, beleive I can have it - I have Love + happiness - and not doubt and question all the good in my life - knowing I deserve it all and more.

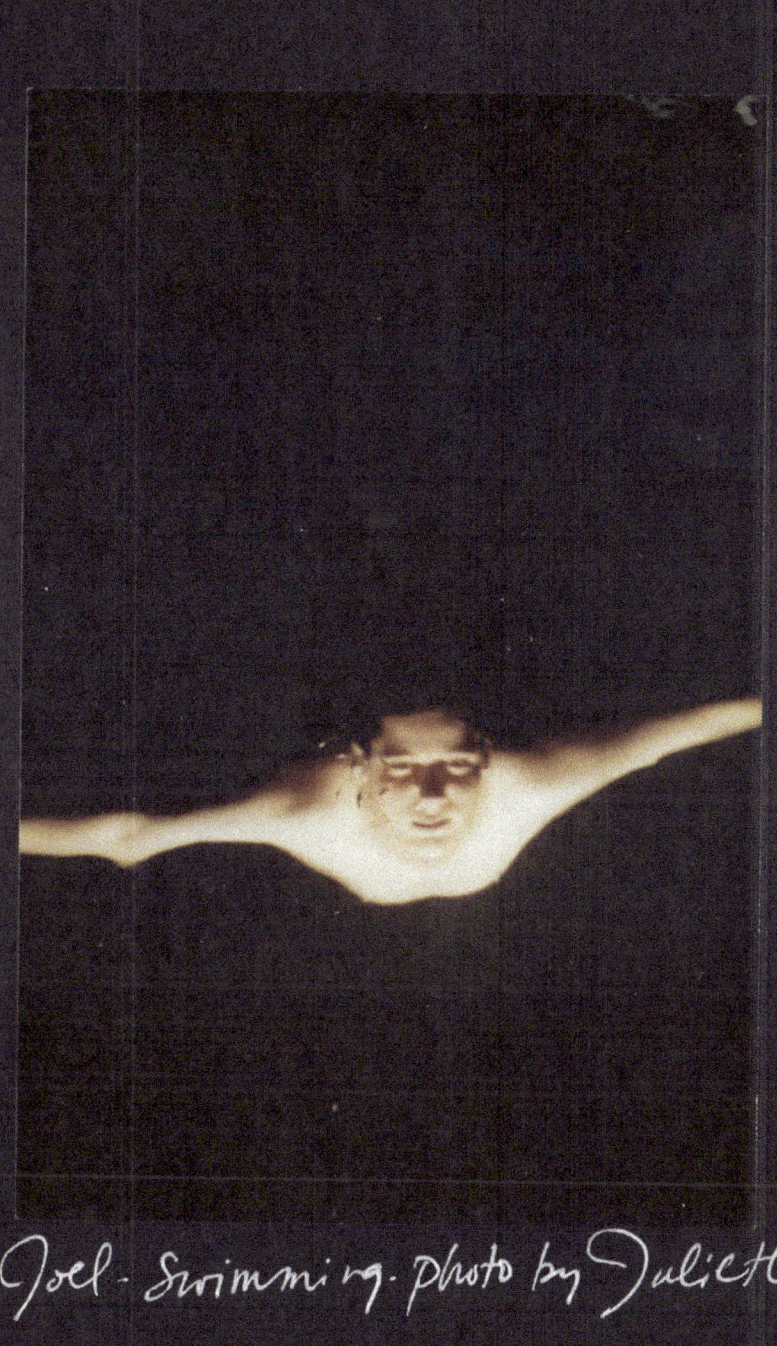

Joel - Swimming. photo by Juliette

# JUNE 2023

Every morning I wake up and take a little blue pill. It's a numbing pill.

A pill to help take the edge off of my anxiety as I move throughout this world.

This world is not for the faint of heart. Why do we feel the need to numb ourselves?

What is wrong with this life <u>and the world we live in</u> that makes numbing yourself necessary to survive?

I think it's just a numbing pill to dull my spark.

<u>I'm going to</u> start believing that I can ask for what I desire, believe I can have it.

Have love and happiness - and not doubt and question all the good in my life,

Knowing I deserve it all and more.

# ITALY, OCTOBER 2023

Good Girls
Are not supposed to be hungry
To want things
Food, sex, or their body
They are not supposed to desire,
or get excited
Or open their mouths real wide
Or have opinions
Good girls are supposed to wait,
Patiently
For permission that is never coming
That will never be granted
From outside forces
Why do you feel guilty
Young one?
For accepting a gift
For speaking up
For saying 'I want that"
For being who you are
Why do you say yes when you mean no?
Why do you lower your voice in a crowded room?
Refuse to live your joy?
These rules we struggle to live by,
Whose rules are they, anyway?
Did we have a part in making them?
I have learned life is short.
So-
Permission Granted
Eat the pasta, define your life
Make your choices
You do not have to be good.
I only need you to be free
So I can be free too.
xo, J.

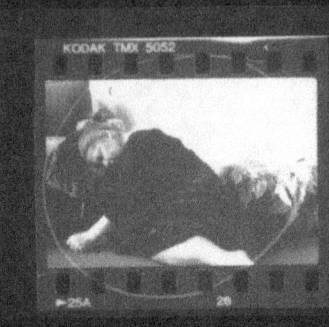

Rest, my dear girl. We have
a lot of work to do. First - feed
your soul and your spirit - because
you are the only one who
will take care of you.

lane. - so I can control + identify
you. So I can predict what
you will do next + be comfortable
with you who you are.
   I remember one time my mom said
"you have guts" - her way of sayin
   I was brave - and my brother
said I was bold. I want to
embrace who I am - because
like Kimk said - "when will I
ever get to be myself." The
image, brains - bussiness +
justice minded - person - we all
have dualities that can co-exist

   Whatever the reason - I am ali
and I want to be alive while I
alive.
         xo I

**10/23**

*Would I rather have her approval, or her bravery?
I feel like I want to say - stop hating yourself
so much, because I am what you made - I am you.

I am a product of the examples you set. How can I
be constantly told to hit the brakes and the gas
at the same time?

'Don't shine too bright.'
'Why don't you do something with your life?'
'I see you're not doing Nutrisystem anymore.'

Not good enough, skinny enough, smart enough.
Not enough.
Never, ever,
**ENOUGH.**

Some of these above may or may not be direct
quotes from my Mom.

I'll just leave that here.

xo,
J.

- young one.
- For accepting a gift
- For speaking up
- For saying 'I want that'
  - For being who you are

- Why do you say yes when you mean
- Lower your voice in a crowded room
- Refuse to live your joy
- These rules we struggle to live b
    who's are they, anyway
  - Did we have a part in making the

- If have learned life is short

- So
- Permission Granted
- Eat the Pasta · Define your life
- Make your choices

- You do not have to be good.
  ___
- I only need you to be free
- So I can be fr

- Good Girls
- Are not supposed to be hungry
- To want things
- Food, sex, their body
- They are not supposed to desire, or get excited.
- Or open their mouths real wide
- Or have opinions

- Good girls are supposed to wait,
- Patiently
- For permission that is never coming
- That will never be given
- From outside forces

- Why do you feel guilty

# Part Three

*"...And now that I don't have to be good I can be free"*
-Unknown

# everything

wrestling my inner demons  - this need to
please runs deep.
this scarcity, this belief i need to conform
or perish

fear of letting go of my safe life
fear of relying on myself
she said i take care of myself
then why am i so miserable?
is it because of the war inside of me
is is because i'm constantly abandoning myself
is it because i can't stop complaining or
playing the victim
afraid to be a hero
afraid to be bothered
with expectation
with responsibility
it's easy to hide in the shadows when you are
constantly pointing fingers at everyone else

so, how do you become the hero?

brene brown once said:
"when you put out your hand for something that
you want, and continuously get it slapped,
there is trauma to that"

you are afraid of your own power, she said to
me.
what does that mean
it means everything
It means everything.

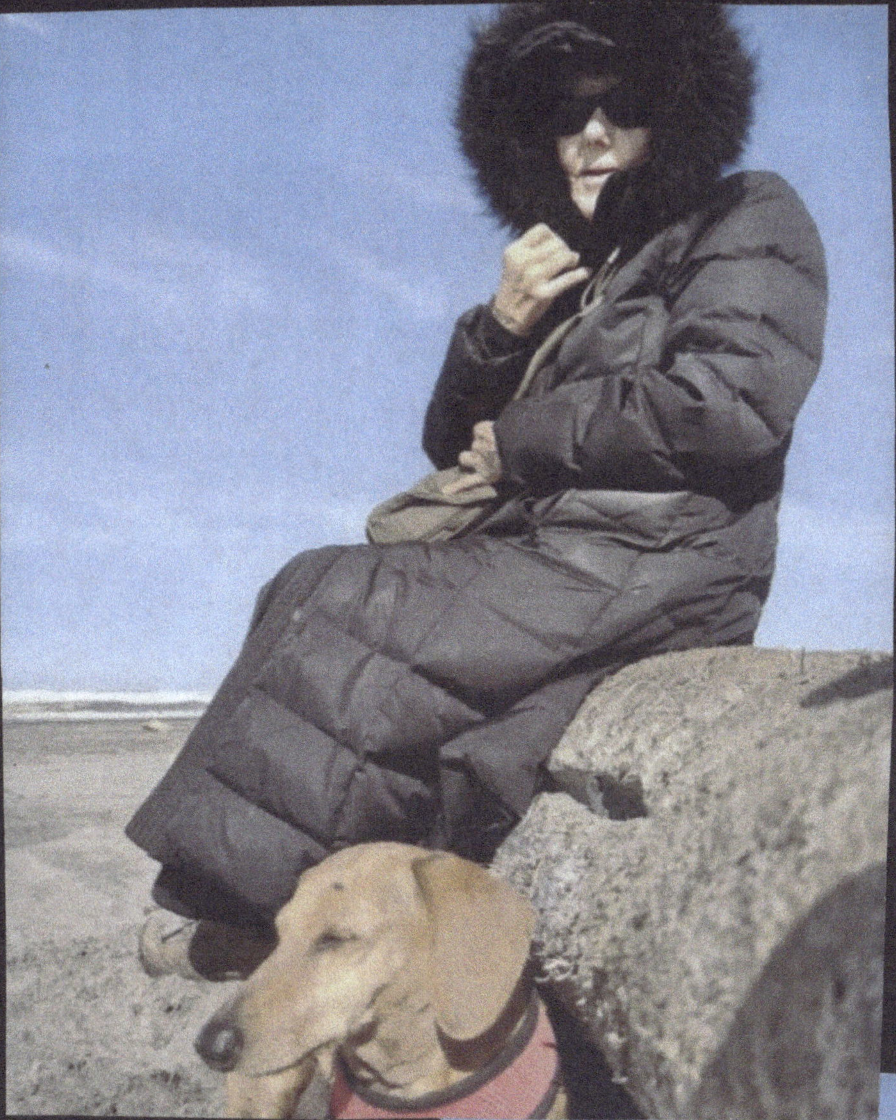

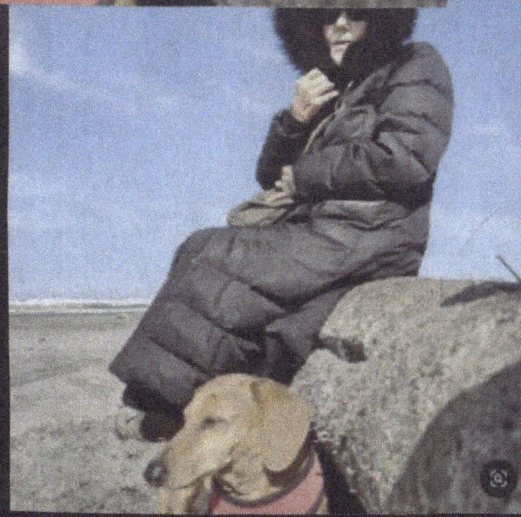

Mom. 2021 (?) - Photo by JoelRi

# BADASS

People always ask me
How I have the courage to
travel alone. I reply "my mom
travels alone - all over the world -
It comes naturally to me."

I suppose I could say the
same thing regarding my
creative adventures.
It comes naturally to me.
I guess I'm more alike
my mother than I thought.

**BADASS**

People always ask me how I have
the courage to travel alone.

I reply:

"My Mom travels alone - all over
the world - it comes naturally to
me."

I suppose I could say the same
thing regarding my creative
adventures.

It comes naturally to me.

I guess I'm more like my mother
than I thought.

My love of art, books, and travel
comes from her.

"(AND)
"now that I
don't have to

be good I can

be free."

(-unknown)

I saw this fellow diner in a restaurant tonight here in New York.

As I casually gazed over my side salad I saw her green sweatshirt boast in bold letters "Be Happy, It's OK."

I took a deep breath and let it out slowly as I thought to myself

"That is exactly what I needed."

If there is any moral to this story - that is it.

Four little words found on the back of a strangers sweatshirt.

Interesting how I travelled so far to find what was right in front of me.

## Free Woman

It took a while
For me to thaw
Under the flames
Of a new Belief.

For the first time
I held my soul
Like the precious
One that it was.

I spoke to it
and I set it free
To do what it came here to do,
To be who it came here to be.

I gave it permission
To go on a journey
and touch the lives
of all the other souls
Who needed it.

I gave her permission to be free
For the first time since arriving
In this place.
To see what it was like to create heaven on Earth

To fully realize for the first time that
all this struggling was just an excuse
to merely Survive.

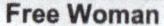

free woman

— the alternative
(alternate) option to
gratitude and Joy
is a waste of your time —
because it doesn't go
anywhere, there is
no resolution — if only
for a moment. Then
you look for your next
hit.
                XO J.

# i don't care

what they say
or if i have permission
to go my own way
to do my own thing
your approval does not equal a
    green light for me
i do what i want
i do what i please
i let myself desire and more
    and breath
no need to edit
no need to shrink
i am here to live a life that wil
    make you think

Oh, I can do that too
i can be free – (forget the murmurs
    of society)
i will make out
i will dance
i will laugh
no need to be scared
no need to behave

**i don't care**

what they say
or if i have permission
to go my own way
to do my own thing
your approval does not equal
a green light for me
i do what i want
i do what i please
i let myself desire
and move
and breathe
no need to edit
no need to shrink
i am here to live a life
that will make you think
oh, i can do that too
i can be free
i will make art
i will dance
i will laugh
no need to be scared
## no need to behave
no need to edit myself
now is the time

i am **BRAVE**

NYC - June 2023

I saw this fellow diner in a restaurant tonight here in New York. As I casually gazed over my side salad I saw her sweat shirt said in huge block lettering —

"Be Happy, It's ok."

I took a deep breath + let it out slowly as I thought to myself —

"That is exactly what I needed."

If there is any moral to this story - that is it.

4 words found on a green strangers sweat shirt.

Interesting how I traveled so far to find what was right in front of me.

Life is sweet — or so they say —
The Lord giveth — and he
taketh away. What I have
learned in my long and
short, fast and slow time
on planet earth is to be
grateful. for all the things
you could possibly think of.
Big. small — tall, short —
upsidedown, backwards —
forwards. It doesn't matter
The other thing is — look
for Joy, not happy (ness)
This is something I heard recently
Joy is the Journey. Happiness is

## SEPTEMBER 2023

Life is sweet, or so they say.
The Lord giveth - and he taketh
away. What I have learned in my
long and short, fast and slow time
on planet Earth is to be grateful,
for all the things you could
possibly think of.

Big, small, tall, short, upside
down, backwards- forwards.  It
doesn't matter. The other thing
is - look for Joy, not happiness.
This is something I heard recently
- joy is the journey. Happiness is
the destination.

Enjoy the journey. The alternative
path to gratitude and joy is a
waste of your time. Because it
doesn't go anywhere, there is no
resolution - if only for a moment.

xo J.

## SEPTEMBER 24, 2023

I (we) got some bad news the other day. It's not the reason he will leave the planet, the doc says.

Whew! Thank God!

But it got us thinking how precious life is, how fragile we are and Yes - this does end.

Just when things seemed to be flowing our way.

But what a gift - this reminder of life's brevity, and to be grateful for each day.

What a reminder to not get too attached to anything.

# Summit Fever

Do you ever get summit fever?
You've started a project - and you
ain't stop until its complete.
You get going, and get on a high.
I think thats what happens
to me - I get started and just
push push push -
I'm so excited about seeing
the final product I dont
stop & breath.
"Sometimes I dont know
why I go to extremes"
                    - Billy Joel

## SUMMIT FEVER

Do you ever get summit fever?
You've started a project -
and you can't stop until it's
complete.
You get going, and get on a high.
I think that's what happens to me
-
I get started and just push push
push -
I'm so excited about seeing the
final product that I don't stop
and breathe.

THE POINT OF LIFE IS SIMPLY
LOVE AND GRATITUDE.

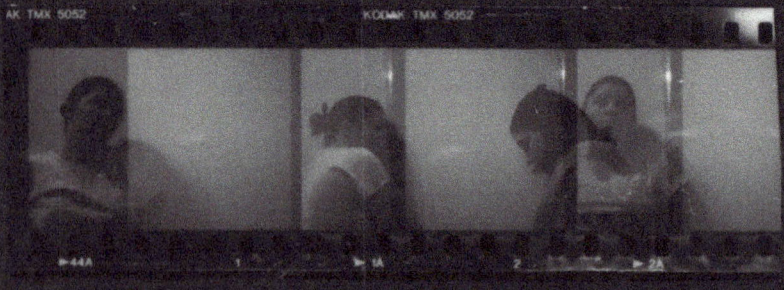

"The Point of Life is
Simply:

Love & Gratitude"

## BRAVERY

Would you rather have bravery
so you can go your own way, or
confidence handed to you on a
silver platter?

Bravery despite or because of your
own circumstances?

I often wish I could go to my
neighbour and ask for a cup of
confidence, like I was asking for
a cup of sugar.

Do you think they would have some
on hand that they could spare so
I could make my one of a kind
pancakes?

Just kidding, I don't make
pancakes.

Sept. 24, 2023

I (we) got some bad news the other day. It's not the reason he will, the planet, the doc says.
leave

whew! Thank God! But it got us thinking - how precious life is. How fragile we are - and yes. this does end.

Just when things seemed to be flowing my way -

But what a gift - this reminder of lifes brevity, and preciousness. What a reminder to not get too attached to anything.

XO I.

Young women receive so many mixed messages:
"Go for your dreams, be independent" but -

"not too independent - you've got bills to pay, and contributions to make."

"Use your talent - but don't try too hard - don't dream too hard or shine too bright - for fear of making others feel bad."

I don't want you to be let down when you are inevitably rejected.

**AFTER ALL- YOU ARE ONLY A GIRL...**

**WHO ARE YOU TO BE BRILLIANT, EMOTIONAL, FEELING, BRIGHT, POWERFUL?**

Be realistic, play by the rules - fit in.

**DON'T ROCK THE BOAT.**

Cheryl Strayed said
"How wild it was to let it be."
I am starting to understand
that you have to let people,

things, nature, whatever be
what and who they are.
No sense in trying to
make someone or something
act or mold themselves to

## CHERYL STRAYED SAID:

"How wild it was to let it be."

I am starting to understand that
you have to let people, things,
nature, whatever be what and who
they are.

No sense in trying to make
someone or something act or mold
themselves to what they are not.

They will just return to their
original shape.

° would I rather have her approval
or her bravery. I feel like I want
to say - stop treating yourself so much,
because I am what you made -
I am you. I am a product of the
examples you set.   How can I
be constantly told to hit the brakes
and   the gas at the same time.
"Don't shine too bright" / "why
don't you do something with your
life?" /   "Put some makeup
on" / "Don't be so selfish" /
"...I see nutrisystem isn't working
for you anymore."

    Some of these above are direct
quotes from my mother.
            xo - J.

Sun, web/et maybe

Young women receive
So many mixed messages-
"Go for your dreams, be
independant" but-
"not too independant -
you've got bills to pay."
"Use your talent - but
maybe don't try too hard
-don't dream too hard
because I don't want you
to be let down when you
are inevitably rejected."
- after all, you are only
a girl. Be realistic,
play by the rules- fit
in. That is how you
will be happy - or at least
how you keep from getting
hurt.

Don't shatter this box you were
put in.

That is how you will be happy -
comply.
**BE COMPLIANT.**

That is how you will survive, and
keep from getting hurt.

But what about sitting with my hot
loneliness?

My sadness?
My discomfort?

**BE BRAVE ENOUGH TO TRUST IN YOUR
BRILLIANCE.**

## MY STEPMOM PASSED AWAY RECENTLY.

A few years ago - after my father passed, she told me that she wanted to meet a man and travel the world.

She never did.

I want to travel _for_ her.

I want to take her around the world.

Where do you think she'd like to go?

I'll ask her.

I think I'm learning that regardless of good or bad things happening to you - acceptance is the only truth.

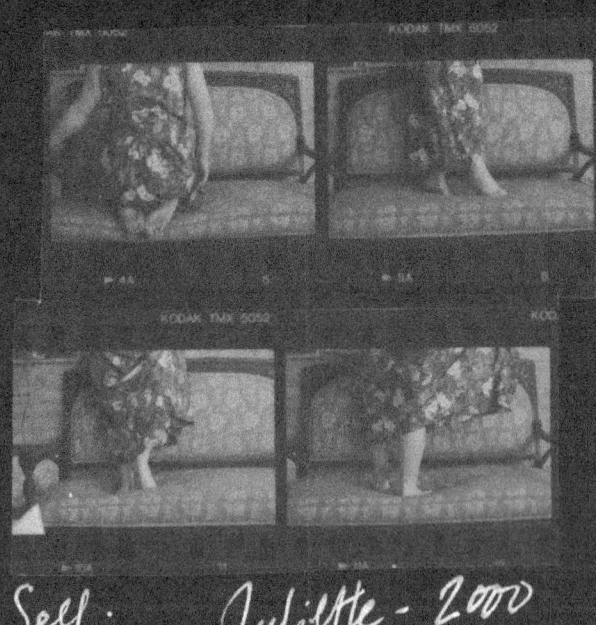

Self.     Juliette - 2000

How do you crawl under your own skin
when you are standing in it?
How do you operate on your own heart, and change
your own mind?
I mean, don't you need someone to help you with
that?  Don't you need a degree or something?
Or to at least consult with the experts first.
How do you achieve love of ones self
when all you've ever been taught to do is
protect it from getting hurt, and to serve
everyone but your self.
In order to be loved you must be Self-less.
Meaning "without a self."
In order to be loved you must serve.
You must put yourself last.
You must never, ever, ever be Self ish.
In other words, you must never be like your self.
You must never like your self, either.
So what is the answer?
I'm not sure, but I will find out and report
back.

## MERCY

i told someone
my plans
the other day
and they
proceeded to
foist all of
their fears
upon me

the way
the world
does

while i
appreciate
the act
of love
they attempted
to protect
me with

it was not
what I needed
anymore
i had let

my shield go
i had decided to
love myself
and that was
all i needed
to have mercy
on my dreams
and soften
the agenda
of the world

to let it
melt away
in a pool
at my feet

an armour
for someone else
to pick up
on another day

i was done
using mine
forever

## WITH ABANDON

am i allowed to have a good life?
should I pause
should I freeze
and brace for impact
every time I turn around
i am always
waiting for the other shoes to
drop
for someone
to tell me I am not allowed
to have that
to get my hand slapped,
every time I reach my hand out
for something i want
will that take the pain away
if i don't desire anything
if i don't expect anything
if i don't wish for anything
i have nothing to lose
maybe i think i can't take the
pain
maybe i am capable of more than i
think
maybe the pain of not reaching is
much bigger than living
with abandon

my stepmom passed away
recently. A few years ago
after my father had passed
she told me that she wanted
to meet a man and travel the
world. She never did. I want
to travel for her.

I think I'm learning that
regardless of good or bad things
happening to you - acceptance
is the only truth.

_____

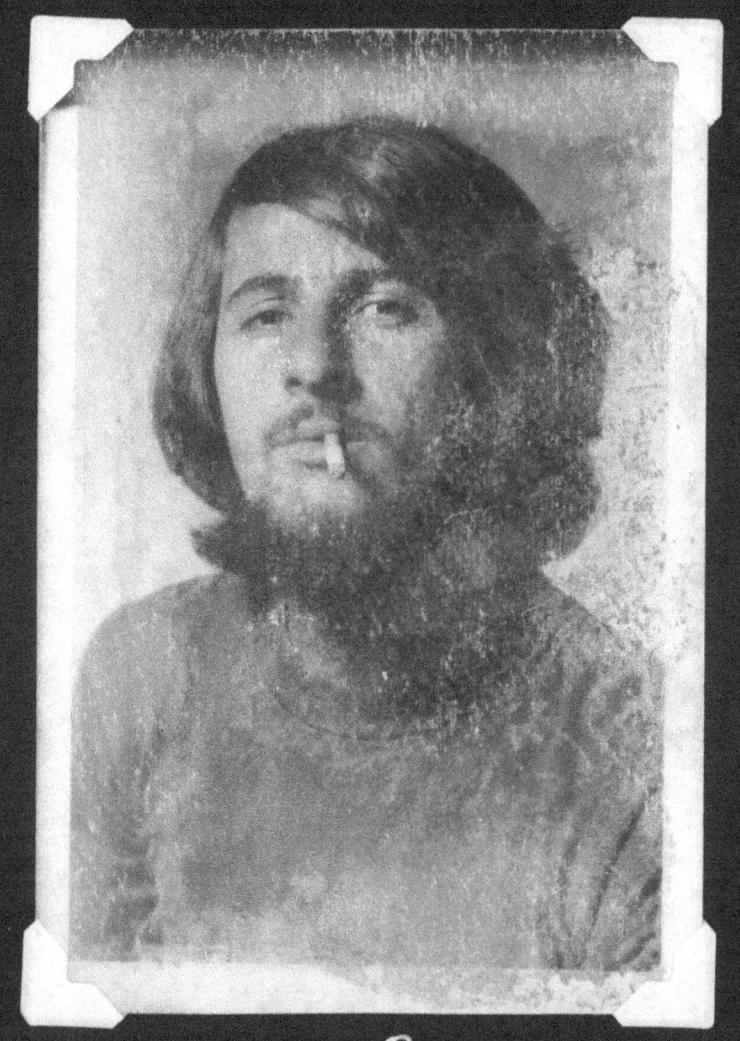

Self p.    — Remi Ricci —

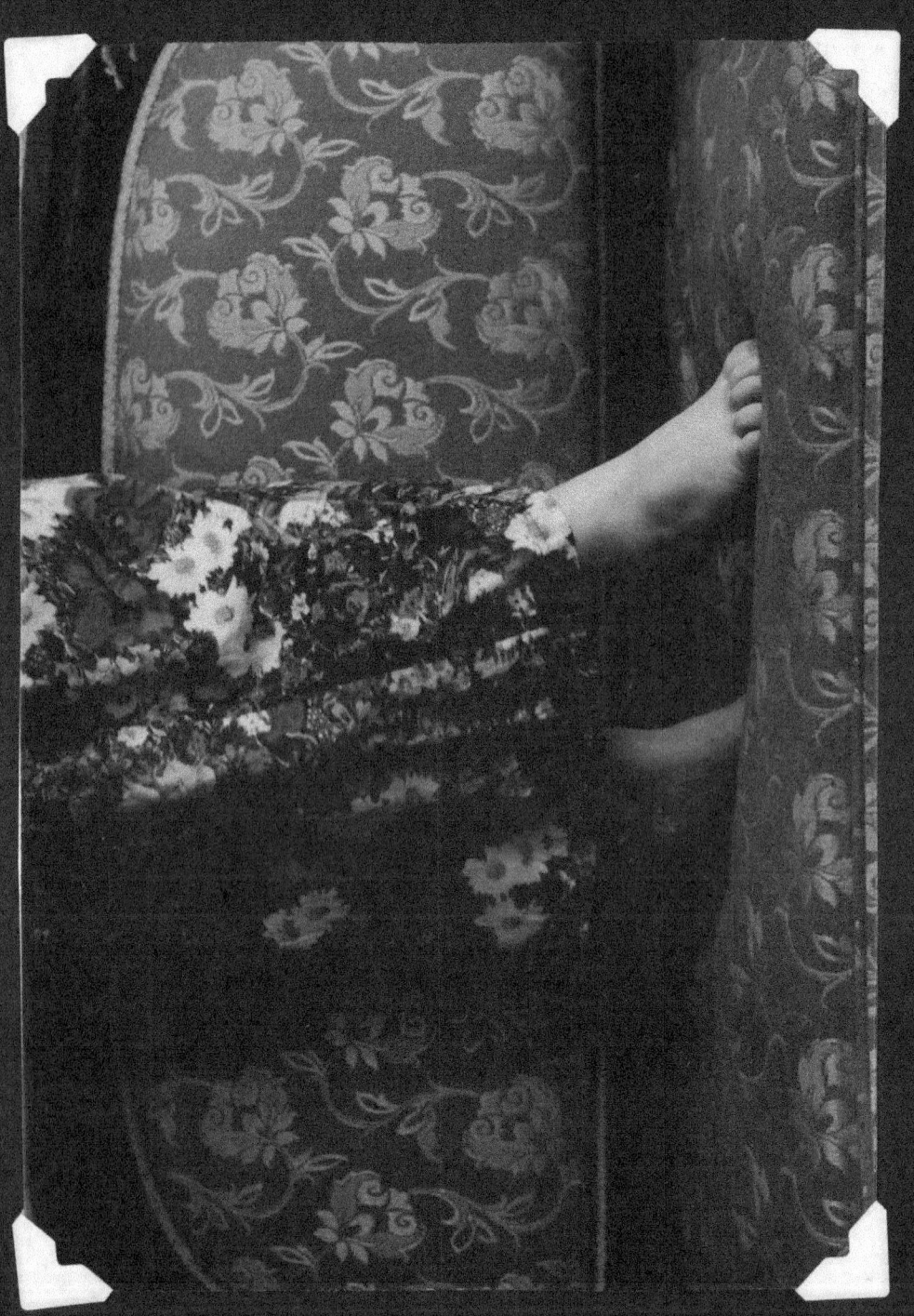

**THE** week before Christmas
before my first trip to the
Philippines
my mind went to a really dark
place
i was definitely grieving the loss
of my stepmom.

i had a **NIGHTMARE** that someone
told me
not to create my book
and that was the scariest thing
i could have dreamt.

i told my therapist about it and
she asked my why
why was that such a scary notion?

the words just fell out of my
mouth -
'it's because i'm a writer
it's who i am,'
and not fulfilling that is
the scariest thing of all.

Juliette Rici 2014

Let me go. Set me free. I just want
to see every thing.

　　I am not your mirror — so look
away. I don't have the answers
to the questions that you've been

'Set me free' by Juliette Ricci

So i went to the
bookstore yesterday
and i realised
they had run out of
self-help books
for me to buy
either i am cured
or i have bought
them all
already.

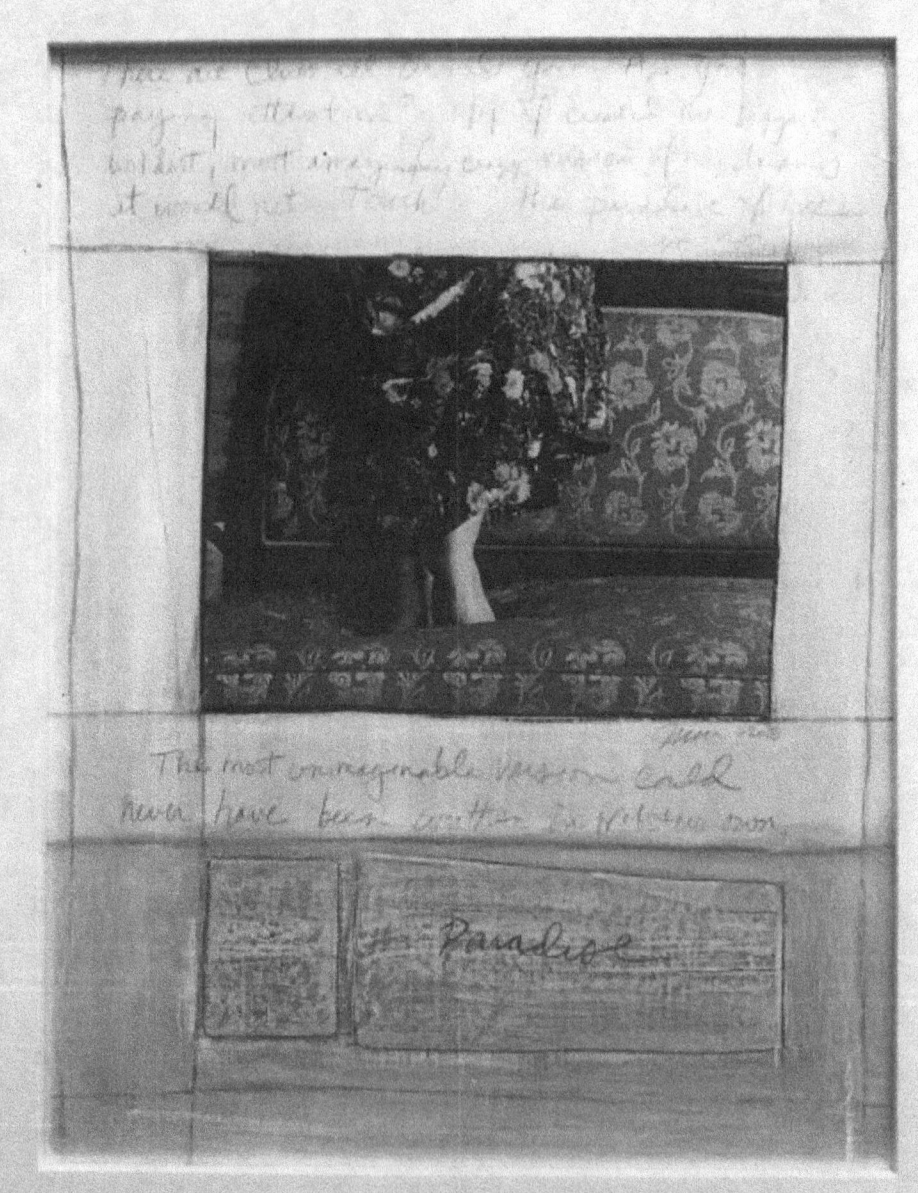

'Paradise' by Juliette Ricci

Follow your bliss . . . .

# TIME

sit right there
and tell me things
time is precious

time is precious
she whispered

as she stretched
her luscious arm
towards me.

I can't.
i can't capture
this feeling in a
bottle, but maybe
in a ribbon
that i wrap
around my long,
brown hair.

i wouldn't trade the
precious memories

i don't question
anymore
their value
they are, my dear
worth more than diamonds
or gold.

they are, in fact
priceless.

my father used to
say - "I've been all
around the world and
parts of Snohomish
County."

me too Dad, me too.

## WILDEST DREAMS

set me free
i got stuck
i need permission
to live my life
to live my dreams
follow my bliss

tired of getting bruised
hitting my head
against the wall
trying to escape
forgiveness and fate

set yourself free
forgive yourself
give yourself permission
you are the only one
that can
achieve these things

go live your life
live your wildest dreams
be like water
it does what feels right
a powerful force
calm as the night

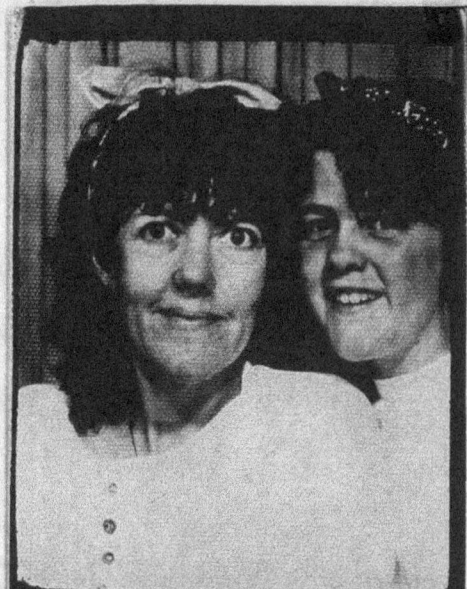

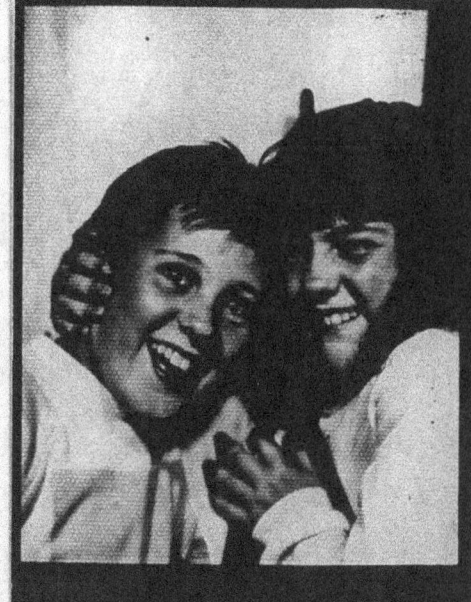

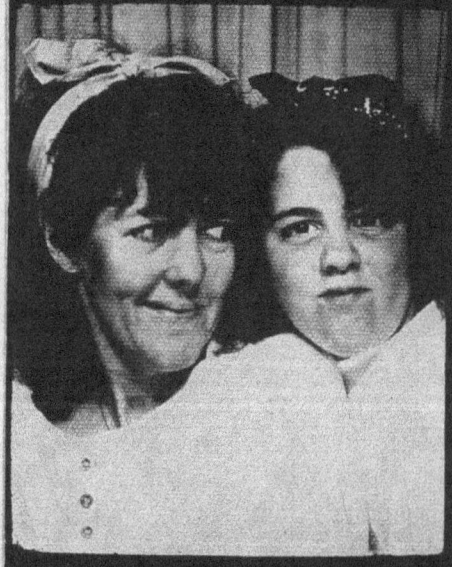

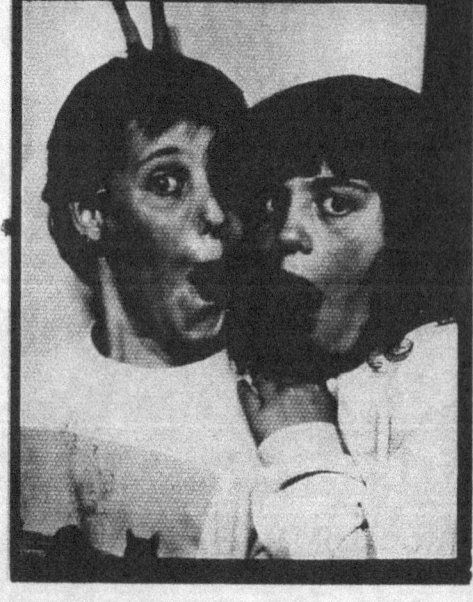

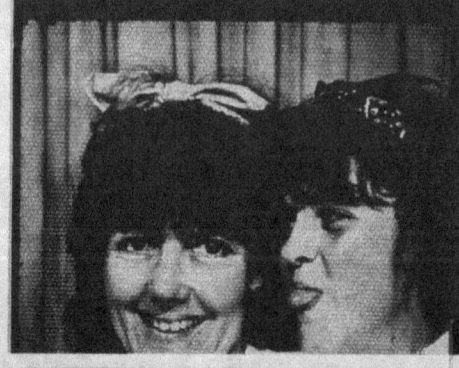

Mom + Julie        1        Joel + Julie

## EPILOGUE

My brother's letter said it all -
all those years ago.  But I had to
discover it for myself.

I have overcome many hurdles,
and am moving on by putting down
all that fear and doubt and
resentment.

I was given.

Carrying all these years.

I determine my worth, decide what
I believe in, and who I love,
unconditionally.

It's your life, live it.

XO
J.

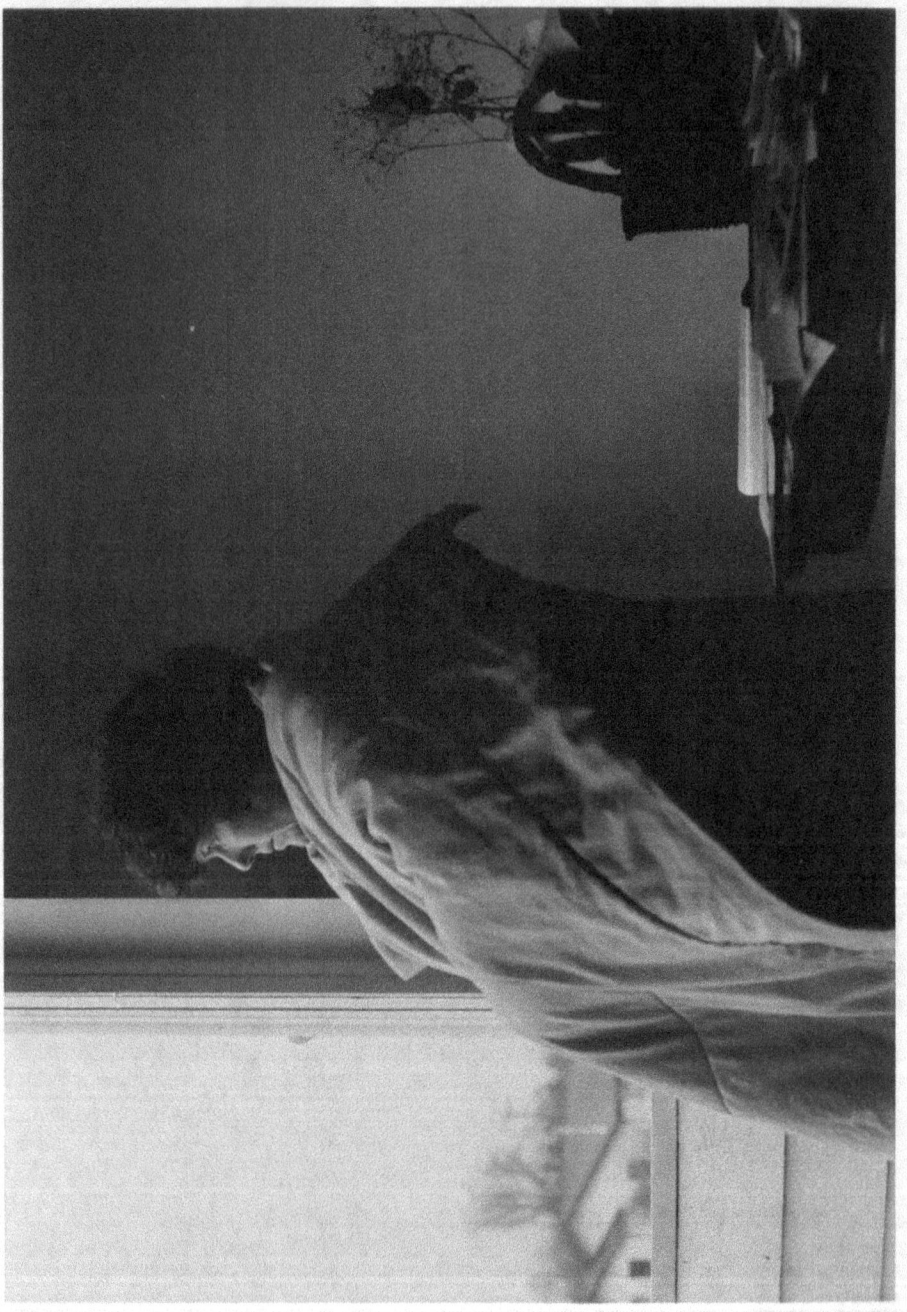

# Epilogue.

My brothers letter said it
all — all those years ago.
But I had to discover it
for myself. I have overcome
many hurdles, and am moving
on by all putting down all
that fear + doubt I was
given — carrying all these years.

I determine my worth, decide
what I believe in, and who
I love, unconditionally.

It's your life. Live it.

Xo, J.

## FOR GAYLE AND URSULA.

I do it for you.
I will travel and carry you
with me.
Thinking of you - every step
of the way.
I will carry you in my heart
and let that guide me,
always.

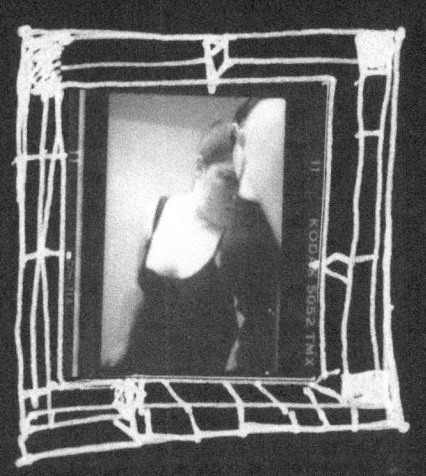

For Gayle and Ursula □
I do it for you.
I will go travel, and carry
you with me. Thinking of
you - every step of the way.
I will carry you in my heart

## ACKNOWLEDGEMENTS:

To my fierce and ever talented graphic designer - Sarah Westby. Thank you for pushing me to do the first book, and for joining me on this journey.

To my dear friend Jennifer MacLean- Thank you for always encouraging me to dream big, and for all of your support.

To my dearest Husband Ron: I love you, always. This lifetime and the next and the next.

To my amazing and supportive book coach, Jocelyn Lindsay. You are the best, and I could not have done this without you.

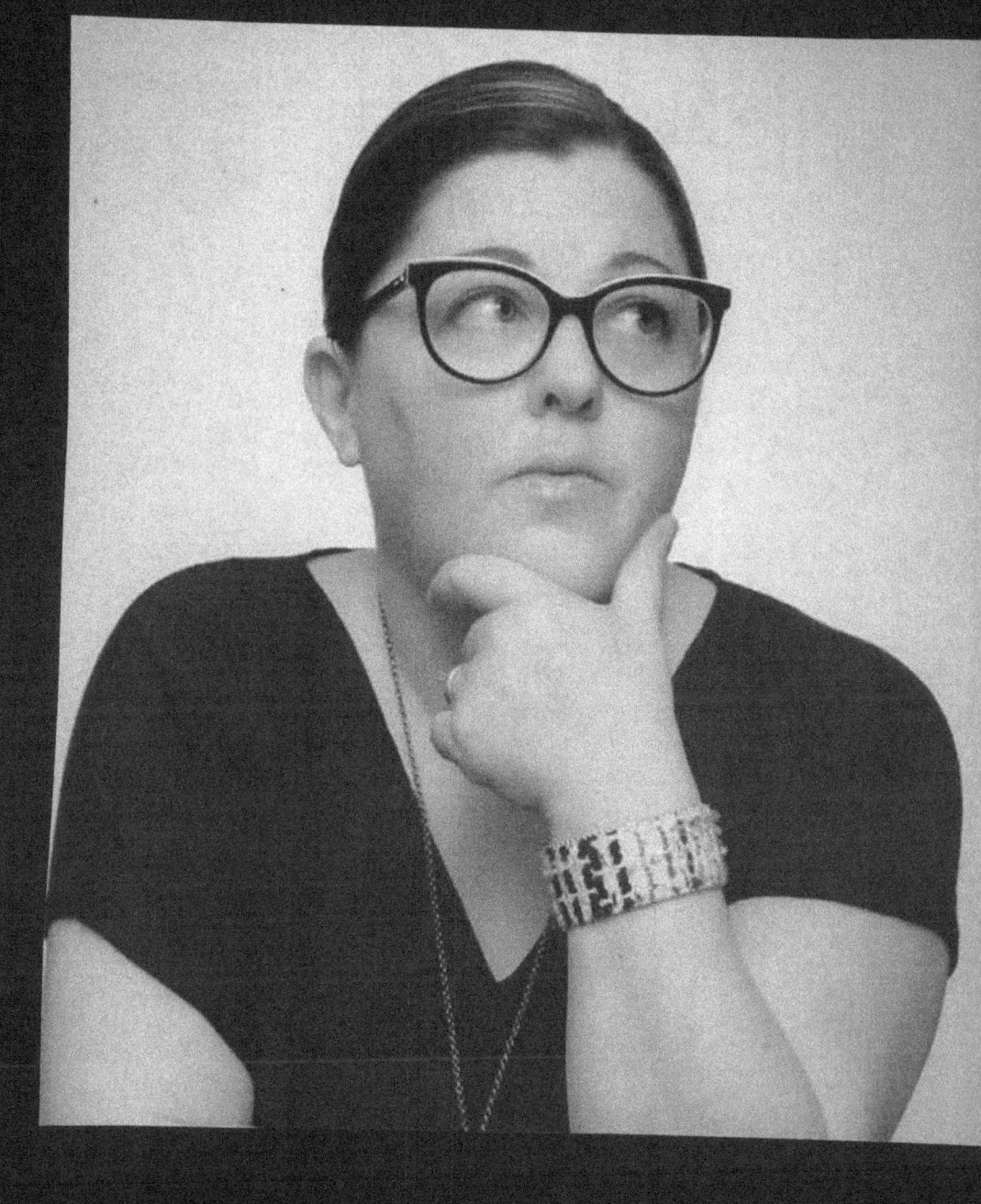

## <u>ABOUT JULIETTE:</u>

Juliette Ricci Lagman is an artist and writer from the Pacific Northwest. She has been painting in her unique mixed media style combining color, text, and image for over 20 years. A graduate of The School of the Art Institute of Chicago, she holds a Bachelor of Fine Arts Degree.

Her first book of prose and artwork: The Juliette Letters, Confessions of an Artistic Mind was published in 2019. She is so delighted to share this book, her first visual memoir with you - Be Like Water.

The Visual Memoir process has been instrumental to her healing and she hopes to continue to create future books in this style. She lives with her husband and cats in a very small but love filled home.

For more info please visit her website *juliettericcilagman.com*